Have You Told All?

Inside My Time with Narconon and Scientology

Lucas A. Catton

Copyright © 2013 Catton Communications

All rights reserved.

ISBN: 978-0615768724
ISBN-13: 0615768725

DEDICATION

This book is dedicated to the brave men and women who dare to take a stand for truth and humanity, and to those who aren't afraid to admit when they have made mistakes.

CONTENTS

	Acknowledgments	i
1	The Bait	1
2	Experiencing Narconon as a Student	6
3	Becoming a Scientologist	28
4	Joining Staff at Narconon	32
5	Becoming President of Arrowhead	51
6	Just Another Extension of the Church	63
7	Stepping Down as President	97
8	Finishing Staff	116
9	Moving to Clearwater	134
10	Leaving Clearwater, Sort of	155
11	Disconnection Hits	184
12	Deciding to Speak Out	193
	Conclusions	199

INTRODUCTION

I was a Scientologist for 12 years and contributed to many Scientology-related activities. I was introduced to the organization primarily through its rehabilitation program Narconon, and worked with them for over ten years in various capacities, including as president of their flagship facility in Oklahoma called Narconon Arrowhead.

There were many highs and lows that I experienced as part of that group, though in the end the negatives outweighed the positives and leaving proved to be a challenge. It cost me my marriage, hundreds of thousands of dollars, many years of anguish and dozens of good friends who disconnected from me when I was officially declared a suppressive person (An SP is Scientology lingo for being evil or ex-communicated) for standing up for truth, honesty and doing the right thing.

As the months have unfolded, I have continued to peel away the layers of embedded judgmental thoughts and other mental traps that I got myself into by being a part of these organizations. After more than a year I finally started to publicly speak out, and found that there are many, many details of personal experiences that they don't want others to know about. Part of my healing process and taking responsibility for participating is to share the truth of those events in order to hopefully help others.

I tried to follow the timeline of significant events as I recalled them, and found many documents verifying my recollection of these events and when they occurred.

1 THE BAIT

My parents have always been very hard-working and honest people. Having children at a young age, I look back at all they accomplished already in their twenties and early thirties and marvel at what they managed to pull off and work through.

My father worked in the dental management field, something he pursued almost immediately after graduating from St. Thomas University in Minnesota. His father was a dentist and one of the early pioneers of having larger group dental practices rather than single doctor-managed offices.

My dad received training to use a dental management software in the early 80's from a company called Quality Systems, Inc. (QSI) and also became a certified trainer for using the software. Not long after that he got a call from QSI about a group dental practice in Arkansas looking for someone who could manage them who knew the software. So, right before I started kindergarten, we moved from St. Cloud, MN down to Fayetteville, AR.

The lure of a good-paying job, new house, new car and southern warmth didn't last very long, as my dad found some things the doctors were doing that he couldn't support. We lived there only a year and wound up moving to Tucker, GA, where he took a job managing another office for a larger group dental practice. We stayed a bit longer, living in two different houses while I finished first and second grades, then moved up to Maryland in a job transfer. I spent my third grade year at two different schools first in Gaithersburg and then in Columbia.

As kids, moving around didn't seem too difficult. My brother and I always made friends with other kids in the neighborhoods we lived in, and sometimes it was more adventurous than disruptive to move to a new place. Thankfully that social pliability was put to use another time because the struggling dental company folded and we moved yet again - this time back to Georgia.

Two doctors wanted my dad to be the president of the company and pull it up from bankruptcy to profitability because of his experience and competence level. It was a huge job, but he was eager to prove himself and it was an enormous challenge. My mom started working with him at that time as well. By then I was in fourth grade and we were living in Woodstock, GA, which is where we finally stayed until both my brother and I finished high school.

It was during this time with the resurrection of the dental offices that they decided to hire a management consulting company. Somehow they settled on a company called Executive Power, which was, unbeknownst to them at the time, run by Scientologists. It was a company that specializes in teaching businesses the organizational policies written by L. Ron Hubbard for his churches that are then applied to other types of businesses. They fall under the church front group known as the World Institute of Scientology Enterprises (WISE).

It was during this consulting that Executive Power suggested to my dad that he improve himself personally by getting auditing (Scientology counseling sessions) from someone in the local Atlanta area named Mary Rieser. And so it began.

My dad wound up not only helping that company become profitable but also went on to operate his own dental offices successfully, and was awarded "Entrepreneur of the Year" by Executive Power. He later started working with them for a bit while the owner, John Stewart, went down for some special auditing at Flag in Clearwater. Flag is the name of the Scientology church there and is where parishioners from all over the world travel to as their spiritual headquarters.

When John returned, he used "the Tech" (as Scientology is colloquially called amongst members) against my dad and conned him into working for free for a period of time. This was one of the first major indicators of how corrupt the organization is and its members can be. It was at least enough for my parents to keep the church at arms length for many years.

I would hear my parents talking about going to see Mary for auditing, doing "the Purif" (Scientology's Purification Rundown sauna sweat-out program, which is also used at Narconon), and starting to use other Scientology terms, but it was never pushed on me.

Then when I was in high school, my parents set up for me to meet Mary and try out some auditing. I had been baptized Mormon at the time, as my girlfriend was Mormon and I was spending a lot of time with her and talking to some missionaries. I remember her being concerned about my going to see Mary and that she was afraid of Scientology for some reason. At that time I hadn't heard anything negative about it at all, and the only reference I had was the exploding volcano commercial for Dianetics I had seen on television.

While I didn't really get involved in Scientology back then, it was the first instance out of many that it would have a negative impact on my relationships.

I would drive down to Mary's office and she would try and go over definitions with me, but I wasn't really in to it. I was more interested in the gimmicky electropsychometer (called an e-meter) and trying to make it do things. Mary would watch the needle on the dial on her side and ask "what was that?", and I'd tell her that I was trying to make it do things. She said it wasn't something to play with, and wound up telling my parents that I wasn't ready or interested.

Fast-forward a couple years and I was a smart-ass college drop-out who liked to hang out with friends and drink a lot. I was working in bars and restaurants, had gotten arrested twice for underage drinking and was generally without direction in life - not unlike many twenty-year-olds. It was no excuse for my behavior, but I also wasn't "an addict".

Then one night I got pulled over by a Sheriff's Deputy after I had been drinking and had an open container in the car. The Deputy was off duty and called another one in to assist him. He proceeded to give me a field sobriety test, which I passed. He then gave me a breathalyzer, which I failed. I told him the truth about my previous arrests and was coherent and had an open and honest conversation with him. He came back and said he decided that he was going to call my parents instead of arrest me. The assisting officer told me I was lucky that he wasn't first on the scene, or he would have already arrested me.

My parents arrived quickly since I was only a couple miles from their home, and one of them drove my car back while I rode with the other. They didn't really want to talk about it. I crashed on their couch and woke mid-morning when they came into the family room and said they wanted to talk to me.

Earlier that morning they had called Mary Rieser and a woman named Christine, both of whom were Field Staff Members (FSMs) for Narconon, specifically in Oklahoma. There were only three centers at that time - one in Oklahoma, one in northern California and one in southern California. Mary and Christine told my parents the best thing they could do for me was to send me to Narconon Chilocco in Oklahoma. My mother asked Christine if that was what she would do with her own child, and Christine said yes. They took their advice and arranged for me to go, all before I woke up.

When my parents spoke to me they said they knew I had a problem and that I should go to this place in Oklahoma to get some things sorted out. They never told me it was a drug rehab, and definitely didn't say it was a Scientology-run rehab. They made it out to be more like a retreat or outward bound-type thing. I was due to start a new job that day and wasn't interested in going on any trips, but at the advice of Christine and Mary they told me if I didn't go then I was no longer welcome in their home and they would call the Deputy back and ask him to arrest me for DUI.

I was shocked, to say the least. Sensing that they were dead serious, and not wanting to get charged with a felony or be cut off from my parents, I agreed to go.

"When?" I asked.

"I already have a ticket booked for you this afternoon," my dad replied.

"And I already have a bag packed for you," my mom added.

That was it. We drove to the airport thirty minutes later. It was the summer of 1998 and I was 20 years old.

2 EXPERIENCING NARCONON AS A STUDENT

Narconon Chilocco was in north-central Oklahoma in an old Native American boarding school between Newkirk, OK and Arkansas City, KS. I flew in to Wichita. I was greeted at the airport by a man in his forties with a sleeveless shirt showing his tattoos, a Boston accent and a lazy or glass eye.
"You Luke?" he asked.
"Yeah," I cautiously replied.
"I'm George," he said, which sounded more like JAWJ.
It was too surreal. We waited for my bag and went to his red and black convertible Dodge pick-up. Yes, a convertible truck. He quickly lit a cigarette and offered me one as well. I gladly accepted to try and calm my nerves while he cranked up Kenny Wayne Shepherd and sped away from the airport.
I came to find out that George Veliskakis was an ex- Hell's Angel and a boxer. Despite his rough edge, though, he was very nice to me. He kindly bought me a cheeseburger before we left Wichita and headed down the back roads to Chilocco.
George told me he was a trainee - that he just finished the program and was about to become a staff member. He explained that clients were called students instead of patients, and that if you did a good program and wanted to help others then you had an opportunity to train for staff. He was training to become an Ethics Officer, which is sort of like a ball-buster in Scientology/Narconon, despite supposedly being there to help you

"keep your ethics in so the Tech could go in" - which translates to keep you in line so the brainwashing can take effect.

After nearly an hour we pulled into a long, straight driveway leading onto the campus, which appeared to be more like a scene from a horror story than a rehabilitation center, with trees lining the driveway, several abandoned buildings and an eerie feeling.

George dropped me off at the little old house used for the withdrawal area. It was there that I met an older guy named Craig Silver who greeted me and went over some initial paperwork. Craig also had a lazy or glass eye. I mention this just because by then it was midnight, I was in the middle of nowhere in a crappy old house with two men older than me who both had lazy eyes in a weird place. It was just a very odd first impression.

Then Craig had me get up on a table that was similar to a massage or chiropractic table. He said he was going to give me an assist. He then started running his hands on my back and chest and down my legs and arms, telling me it would help me. It was pretty benign and was slightly relaxing despite the creepiness of it all.

Soon after that I was put in a room that had two twin beds in it, but I was the only one in that room for the night. There was someone else in the other bedroom. After brushing my teeth and taking out my contacts I climbed in the bed and just stared at the ceiling for a while, wondering what in the hell I was doing there and what was about to happen. I didn't feel like I was in danger, just very much alone. I thought I was in a completely different world.

I slept until very late the next morning, and since I came in completely sober I only had to be in the withdrawal area for that initial day. The campus was less eerie during the day, but looked even more rundown. I was transferred over to the building known as Home 5, which is where all of the student rooms were. It was basically a dorm building, with large locker-room style bathrooms. The guys were upstairs and the girls were on one side of the downstairs. There were only about 50 students at the time, so I was able to have my own room.

Home 5, like the rest of the campus, was old and dirty. The carpet was stained and musty, as were the mattresses. Most of the furniture was broken in some way or another and the bathrooms had black fungus growing in them. It wasn't pretty. Back then the program cost $17,000 and had a ten percent discount if paid in full up front.

After finishing up a couple interviews with some staff, all of whom seemed nice, I was then brought into the course rooms, which were in the basement of the cafeteria. There were three rooms on one side used for doing the course work, and then two saunas on the other side.

As I walked in I saw two self-professed crackheads sitting across from one another engaged in what would have appeared to be a conversation, but didn't make any sense. I thought I was in a mental ward.

"Do birds fly?" the woman asked.

"They fly out of your butt," said the man.

"Thank you," she replied. "Do birds fly?"

Where the hell was I?

Book 1 of the Narconon program teaches people something called Training Routines (TRs). These are supposed to be communication and confront exercises that L. Ron Hubbard developed as a way to start training Scientology auditors. Every Scientologist does TRs.

The TRs are always done with another person, called a twin. When working with a twin one person is usually the coach and the other is considered the student. TR 0 actually has three steps. Why it didn't start with 1, 2, 3, etc. is beyond me, but then again Hubbard loved to randomly assign numbers to things. So, TR 0 includes eyes closed, eyes open, and bullbaiting.

TR 0 eyes closed consists of two people seated in chairs facing each other about three feet apart with hands in your lap. You are supposed to just sit there comfortably, without thinking, twitching, excessive breathing, sleeping, moving or anything. You are supposed to just BE. This is a variation of what many people know as transcendental meditation. You are not to focus on anything, but instead clear your mind and just be there comfortably. You start out doing that for a few minutes, and gradually work your way up to longer periods of time. In order to complete the drill, you have to work up to sitting there for an hour and be monitored by the course supervisor, who gives you a pass or a flunk. If you flunk, you have to start over. Why an hour? I don't know.

TR 0 eyes open is the exact same thing, but you have to keep your eyes open. This time there can be no shifting of the eyes or excessive blinking. If you try not to blink and you appear to be straining you are given a flunk and have to start over. If you blink too fast you are given a flunk and have to start over. Each time building up longer and longer until you go for a one-hour pass again.

TR 0 Bullbaiting is where the student sits there and the coach sits across from you and can say or do anything to try and get a reaction out of you except touch you. People say all sorts of things, including incredibly vulgar and rude comments about your appearance, about sex, about drugs or violence - anything. Sometimes the coach tries to be funny and make you laugh, or other times the coach says things to make you sad or angry - anything to get a reaction.

If you react, you flunk and have to start over. The things you react to are called buttons, and the coach has to keep pushing those buttons over and over again until you stop reacting. These are often used in a sadistic way, especially at Narconon centers. Imagine being a junkie and in less than a week after withdrawing someone is sitting in your face talking about and demonstrating shooting up heroin in his arm. Imagine you are a woman who turned to prostitution to support your crack addiction, and now someone is across from you mimicking giving a blowjob right in your face and talking about your sexual parts and other sexual acts. Imagine you had incredibly low self esteem and someone is berating you for your appearance or how you're a miserable failure at life. Imagine you already had suicidal thoughts (as many substance abusers do at one time or another) and someone is telling you that you're a piece of shit and probably should just have ended it.

This is what happens the first week at Narconon centers. To most people this is the real beginning of the rewiring of their thinking and behavior. You are not allowed to move on with the program until you can sit and have anything in the world said to you without reacting. You cannot retaliate or say anything in return. Once the supervisor feels you are sufficiently not reacting to anything, which is usually after many hours back and forth with your twin, then you go on to the next Training Routine.

TR 1 is supposed to be about delivering a communication. You pick random selections from Alice in Wonderland (yes, always that book) and read them to your twin. If you cannot speak clearly enough, make good eye contact and have your intention received on the other end, the coach says "flunk" and you have to do it again. If you do say these completely oddball sentences well enough, you are acknowledged, thanked or congratulated in some way and then move on to the next sentence.

Here is an example:

Student: "It's a Cheshire cat."

Coach: "Good."

Student: "Off with his head!"

Coach: "Thank you."

Student: "I shan't be much longer."

Coach: "Great."

This again continues for hours back and forth, with the twins taking turns as student and coach.

TR 2 is about giving an acknowledgement. This time the coach reads a line from Alice in Wonderland and the student must give an appropriate acknowledgement to what was said. If the coach feels it wasn't appropriate then you are given a flunk and have to do it over.

TR 2 1/2 (yes, another weird number) is a half acknowledgement. This time the coach reads a line and pauses in the middle. The student is supposed to say something like "go on", "please continue" or "tell me more," etc. and then the coach finishes reading the sentence.

TR 3 is about asking a question until you get it answered, except the only questions allowed are "do birds fly?" or "do fish swim?" and nothing else. If your twin doesn't answer your question, you must say, "I'll repeat the question, do birds fly?" and it doesn't matter what the answer is, even if it is wrong. The point is to get an answer to your question, hence the scenario with the crackheads I mentioned before.

TR 4 uses the same questions, but this time you are supposed to do something called handle originations. An origination is described as something a person says about himself, such as a problem, thought or realization of some sort. You are not allowed to answer one of their questions, just handle their origination and get them to answer your question.

Here is an example:

Student: "Do birds fly?"

Coach: "Nope."

Student: "Thank you."

Student: "Do birds fly?"

Coach: "The sky is pretty."

Student: "I'll repeat the question. Do birds fly?"

Coach: "My mouth is sort of dry."

Student: "As soon as we're done you can get some water."

Coach: "Oh, ok."

Student: "I'll repeat the question. Do birds fly?"

Coach: "How many birds make up a flock?"

Student: "I'll repeat the question. Do birds fly?"

Coach: "Birds fly south in the winter."

Student: "Thank you."

Once again, you switch back and forth with your twin being the coach and the student for hours until finally given a pass from the supervisor.

Sound sort of insane yet? There's more. There actually is not a TR 5, but TR 6 has two parts (go figure).

TR 6 part A has no verbal commands from the student. You are simply supposed to walk your twin around the room by maintaining control with light physical contact, such as one hand on the arm and one behind the back. The coach can try and break your concentration or control by saying things or trying to walk away. If they get away or make you react to what they're saying, you're given a flunk and have to start over. You keep walking this person around the room until the supervisor gives you a pass.

TR 6 part B is the opposite. There is no physical contact, though you are still standing closely and walking along side the person. The commands used are "look at that wall (pointing)," "walk over to that wall," "touch that wall," "turn around," "look at that wall," etc. This goes on and on, back and forth over and over in between two walls. You are not allowed to touch the other person, not allowed to react and not allowed to answer any questions or handle any originations. The only other thing you say is "I'll repeat the command," if they do not do as you ask or "thank you" when they comply with your commands.

TR 7 is just like the previous one but now you must handle originations in addition to it.

TR 8 is infamous. This is where you sit down in a chair and have an ashtray in the chair across from you. You are told at first to pick up the ashtray and then set it down again, thinking the commands in your head though instead of saying them aloud. It is supposed to be about having intention on doing something and then doing it. The next part is you verbally command the ashtray while using your hands, first in a regular voice, and then as loudly as you can by yelling, "Stand up! Thank you! Sit down on that chair! Thank you!" This is done repeatedly. That's right. When someone says you talk to ashtrays in Narconon and Scientology, it is true.

TR 9 is back to the walls. This time you use a combination of all previous TRs together, such as being able to confront another person comfortably, giving commands, handling originations and using necessary physical contact to guide them if needed.

Despite how crazy this all sounds, the underlying part that is much worse is the fact that it is teaching people how to control others and how to allow yourself to be controlled. You wind up becoming more compliant with what you are told to do, which opens up the door to everything else down the road.

When people are told about Narconon on the phone by a staff member or recruiter, they fail to mention any of this. All that is said is that you do exercises to increase your ability to communicate and confront life. Sounds good, right?

Again, this is what every Narconon student and every Scientologist has to go through in the beginning. You are now malleable in the hands of staff members and the teachings and techniques of L. Ron Hubbard.

Although there were clearly odd things going on, most students on the program quickly started to conform, both because of the controlling factor as well as because they learned from those who had been there longer what you had to do in order to move on to the next thing. Most of the people were simply going through the motions to get done. Another thing is that students had to write a success story after completing each part of the program. If you refused to write one then they would assume something was wrong and make you continue on that part. You weren't allowed to go on to the next step unless you wrote some kind of success story.

It was very much like a small school atmosphere, with students ranging from 18 into their 60's. Most of us were in our 20's and 30's though. There were cliques and clashes just like in school, which are phenomena observable in just about any group.

As time went on, the most important parts were the

associations with people - the friendships that were developed while you were sharing these experiences. Those people were what made it actually fun to be there. The program itself was secondary both in reason for staying as well as for actual influence regarding drug or alcohol use. Connections were made with not just fellow students, but also with trainees and staff.

Some of those connections were immoral and even downright illegal, such as sexual contact between staff, trainees and students or smuggling in alcohol and drugs. Much later on I discovered that these were things that were common to all Narconon centers. It is true that all rehabs are subjected to various problems to one degree or another, but other rehabs are not staffed primarily with recent program graduates who only had a few months of sobriety and whose only training was by the facility itself based on L. Ron Hubbard's ideas.

The next part of the program is called the New Life Detoxification Program, aka the sauna program, aka the Scientology Purification Rundown. It is based on the book Clear Body, Clear Mind written by Hubbard. It is done exactly the same in the church as it is in Narconon, but Narconon centers do not use e-meters. Book 2 is a picture book with illustrations explaining what the procedure claims to do.

The concept, developed around 1978, was to rid the body of unwanted stored toxic residues. In Scientology it is supposed to be a spiritual practice, while in Narconon propaganda it is said to eliminate cravings for drugs. Despite some basic studies of toxic metabolites in the body, there have been zero studies to agree with the principles or condone the procedures that Hubbard developed for his sauna cleansing procedure other than those that were funded by or connected to Scientology and Narconon that I am aware of. On the flip side, there are multiple medical evaluations done by doctors to indicate that the sauna program is not only ineffective, but potentially very dangerous.

A regular day in the sauna program includes weighing in and then getting your blood pressure and heart rate recorded. This is followed by consuming niacin (B3) just prior to 30 minutes of aerobic exercise such as running on a treadmill. Niacin levels start at 100 mg and can go up to 5,000 mg in some cases. Niacin can create a heavy flush and itching sensation and high doses have been said to be at risk of causing liver damage.

After the exercise comes another four and a half hours of sweating in a dry-heat sauna in roughly ten to fifteen minute increments, taking a break to cool down or take a cold shower. During this entire time salt and potassium tablets are taken and a lot of water is consumed.

At the end of the sweating process your weight and blood pressure are recorded again. You also take very large amounts of other vitamins and oils and drink a mixture of calcium and magnesium powder dissolved in vinegar and water. This is called Cal-Mag.

Narconon likes to promote that some people re-experience drugs coming back out of their bodies, such as certain thoughts, tastes, smells, feelings, etc. Some individuals believe they feel high again. There is so much placebo effect with this (as with any benefits received from the whole program) that it is hard to tell whether or not what someone reports really happened, or if it was a product of the heat.

For example, the first time I did the sauna program I thought I felt a little dizzy and queasy and attributed this to marijuana coming back out of my system. I had only smoked pot a handful of times though, but wrote it down as being a marijuana "restim" (re-stimulation or occurrence) because I believed in the procedure at the time. Ironically, the dizziness, nausea, etc. that I experienced are also symptoms of being overheated. Years later, when I look back on that, it was absolutely the latter (overheated) and not the original belief or explanation.

According to the Mayo Clinic, the "signs and symptoms of heat exhaustion may develop suddenly, or over time, especially with prolonged periods of exercise. Possible heat exhaustion symptoms include: Cool, moist skin with goose bumps when in the heat; Heavy sweating; Faintness; Dizziness; Fatigue; Weak, rapid pulse; Low blood pressure upon standing; Muscle cramps; Nausea; Headache."

Did I feel good after completing the sauna program? Yes, however I believe I would have had a much better effect not overdoing everything and simply eating right, taking some nutritional supplements and exercising without having to overdose on vitamins and minerals. Toward the end, you're consuming a cup full of pills, most of which simply cannot be absorbed by the body in a day. The vitamins, Cal-Mag and other things consumed wind up creating what I call ass piss. This extreme diarrhea, extreme heat, extreme everything else with the sauna program can cause serious dehydration, despite drinking so much water. It is an over-taxing of the functions of the body.

The sauna program typically lasts about a month. I never went over a month, while some people go for two months. I can't imagine going through that hell five hours per day, every single day, for sixty days in a row.

Book 3 is called The Learning Improvement Course. It is based on three barriers to study that Hubbard supposedly discovered, along with their manifestations and how to overcome them. It's called "Study Tech."

At first it seems pretty simple, until you get into how it is all used in Scientology to reeducate people with Hubbard's new definitions, scales, charts, characteristics, etc.

The three barriers are the 1) Misunderstood Word; 2) Lack of Mass; and 3) Too Steep a Gradient. The first one goes into what they call "word clearing", which means to look up a word, find the correct definition as it is used, use it in sentences, then read the other definitions and use those in sentences and then look up the derivation of the word. Again, this seems at first to be a good thing, but it winds up being tedious and claims things such as all yawns during reading or stumbling while reading aloud are due to misunderstood words. Plus, since the Narconon courses use definitions made up by Hubbard in many cases, you have to word clear his definitions in addition to the ones in a regular dictionary.

Lack of mass means there is a void of reality on what something is. The remedy is said to be to supply the actual thing or a representation of it such as a picture. It also teaches to use "demo kits" and you have to demonstrate out various concepts with small, random objects such as rocks and paper clips. Another type of demonstration use is a clay demo, where you literally have to create entire scenes in clay, labeling each piece, to prove that you understand the concept or definition of a word or idea.

The last part is too steep a gradient, and basically just says that you have to move at the correct pace for each individual, and moving too quickly will leave someone unable to grasp the subject.

All three of these barriers have Hubbard-defined manifestations that students must learn and drill, such as feeling dizzy, bent, squashed, exasperated, tired, sort of spinny or dead, etc. It has been a long-understood observance by scholars of cult characteristics that they often create their own languages or redefine terms and concepts within the language as a means of controlling thought and speech patterns. By implementing the Study Tech early on, the rest of the program is set up to now drill in the students' heads these new concepts and definitions that were created by Hubbard for Scientology. In fact, the average Narconon student leaves the program speaking more Scientology terms than your average Scientologist learns in the same amount of time.

I didn't think much about it back then, though I did sometimes get distracted by the clay demos because I liked making things. It was sort of like playing with Play-Doh all over again! However, the rest of the books then required the use of Study Tech as you went along.

The next book is 4A, which was another go-around of all of the TRs, but this time instead of having to go for one-hour passes on TR0 eyes closed and eyes open, you had to do two-hour passes. If you've never sat in a chair three feet away from another person and stared into their eyes for two hours without moving, consider yourself lucky. I wouldn't recommend it to anyone as a forced practice. Nearly every Narconon student must do this.

Book 4B is about Objective Processes. These are actual Scientology auditing procedures. The book even uses and defines the term auditor in the Scientological sense of "one who listens." Students are taught how to create Session Report Forms and take notes just like in a church, as well as get an "exam" after each auditing session, which is simply someone looking at the person and noting his or her facial and body indicators since there are no e-meters.

Students are twinned up again, where one is the student in session doing the objective processes and the other is the auditor, who asks the questions or gives the commands and notes down the reactions and remarks from the student. Rather than doing it back and forth like most, I had one guy run me through all of them. I believe there were eleven, with number six having three parts. Each Objective Process could last anywhere from a few minutes all the way to several days.

They would include commands such as "Look around here and find something you could permit from going away," followed by "Did you keep it from going away?" There were all kinds of them. Objective number five includes walking around a table with the auditor saying "Touch that table. Thank you. Touch your [indicates body part]". This would continue for hours and include sexual parts after a while (called aberrated body parts in the book).

Overall it took me about two weeks to complete my Objectives, and then I had to run someone else through them, a guy named Todd. What I didn't know at the time was that Todd was sexually abused by his step-father. So later on into it I'm running him on Objective number five and start telling him "Touch that table. Thank you. Touch your penis. Thank you." He winds up having a total breakdown, and the only thing I could do was listen. Auditors aren't allowed to engage in conversation when the person is in session. Plus, I wasn't a counselor or equipped to handle something like that. I didn't care about the rules and tried to console him, to let him know it was okay to talk, that he was safe and that I wouldn't judge anything that happened. After more than an hour, he did finally start to feel better and we took a break. I turned in my session report form for that day and the course supervisor (not a trained counselor, just someone trained in overseeing students while they do their courses) said, "Whoa!" when he saw my notes, "Why don't you guys go take a walk and end off for the day."

That isn't an uncommon experience at Narconon. Often people with substance abuse problems and addictions do have major traumatic events in their lives, and there really aren't trained staff members at Narconon equipped to help them through the breakdowns and deal with those situations. For the most part, all you have is another student and staff members who are only trained in Hubbard's works.

This is also how so many close friendships develop while being a student at Narconon, because it is usually the students who are relied on to get one another through the program. They share common experiences and depend on each other for support. That is where the bonds really start to strengthen. It is also a big reason why a number of student graduates decide to stay on and train to become staff members (though most don't stay long) - to continue to be around people they've developed these relationships with, whether healthy or not. It is often a form of codependency or transference.

Toward the latter half of the program I started waking up early in the morning and I would bring my portable CD player down to the cafeteria and I would write. I loved writing. It was sort of like journaling, but I would write just about anything that came to mind. I would often be the only one in there for an hour or so besides Pat, who was the woman who cooked breakfast every morning. It was a way for me to examine things and collect my thoughts, as well as to reflect on the many personalities and experiences I came in contact with while there. Somewhere there is also a video tape that I made with some interviews of fellow students back then, as I had my parents send a video camera out to me. I remember it being pretty funny, and the genuine humanity of others who found themselves in this one very odd place in the country experiencing these things together.

Book 5 is called the Ups and Downs in Life Course and is all about the 12 characteristics of social and anti-social people, according to Hubbard. It is also the introduction to terms and concepts that he espoused such as a Suppressive Person (SP), a Potential Trouble Source (PTS), Merchants of Chaos (news media, morticians) and more. The basic explanation is that when someone is connected to an anti-social person or SP, they become a potential source of trouble. He theorized that all accidents and illnesses stem only from a PTS condition. In other words, people don't have accidents unless they are connected to a suppressive person and they don't get sick unless they are connected to a suppressive person either. The book also says that people rollercoaster by getting better then worse, better and then worse again.

Hubbard wrote many references on the PTS/SP relationships

that are used at a church, but the core ideas are still taught at Narconon. We had to memorize the 12 social and 12 anti-social characteristics from the book verbatim. After learning all of that each student is given a PTS interview and they are supposed to find out who is an SP in their life that was a contributing factor to their substance abuse or addiction.

Once the SP is identified then they must handle them or disconnect from them. Many times students either come up with names of loved ones on their own or they are suggested to them, especially if they are antagonistic in any way to them being at Narconon rather than some other rehab. So, let's say a guy is at Narconon and his sister finds out about the Scientology connection and then tells him she doesn't trust Scientology, finds stories online and tries to tell him about it. In such a scenario Narconon would suggest that if he couldn't handle his sister to stop saying negative things about Narconon or Scientology then he should disconnect from his sister because she was not supportive of him getting better. This is a root of a much greater manipulation of the PTS/SP doctrine that is used throughout Scientology.

Book 6 is called The Personal Values & Integrity Course. It includes Hubbard's differentiation in definitions of ethics and morals and says that most of society actually has it wrong. You then learn about his definition of life's compartments, which he calls the 8 Dynamics. The 1st Dynamic is yourself and your possessions. The 2nd Dynamic is sex and family, including the sexual act as well as the rearing of children. The 3rd Dynamic is all groups, such as co-workers, teammates, club members, etc. The 4th Dynamic is all mankind. The 5th Dynamic is all other living things including plants and animals. The 6th Dynamic is the material universe, made up of Matter, Energy, Space and Time (MEST). The 7th Dynamic is supposed to be the spirit or spiritual aspect and the 8th Dynamic is said to be infinity or the Creator.

Once you learn about his new definitions for life and living, you are then taught about overts, which are transgressions against oneself or others in the form of commissions (something done) or omissions (something that should have been done). You also learn about withholds, saying that after you have an overt, you then have the withhold of it by not telling someone.

After you have all these new definitions you are then instructed to write down your overts and withholds (called O/W's) in a specific form that names time, place, form and event in as much detail as possible. You are instructed to then share this with the course supervisor, who puts them in the student's folder for the case supervisor to see. This can be extremely humiliating at times to force someone to share his or her deepest darkest secrets in such a manner. While confession may be good for the soul, writing down incredibly thorough details leaves people in a vulnerable state as they re-live it. There is also the fact that they don't actually get any counseling during or afterwards on how to really deal with the things they had to face from their past. All that is gotten is a simple acknowledgement for having written them.

Another problem with the book is that the student may claim to be done, but if the course supervisor or case supervisor doesn't think the person has written enough, he or she must go back and keep writing more to "prove" that everything really was cleaned out. I remember having to dig up petty things to write down because I just couldn't think of the amount they were hoping to get form me. You were supposed to write for days and include overts on all dynamics of any kind. When students were hung up but told to keep writing, they were shown Hubbard's Code of Honor to see if they broke any of those points. The Code of Honor includes things such as "Never desert a comrade in need, in danger or in trouble; Never withdraw allegiance once granted; Never desert a group to which you owe your support; Your self-determinism and your honor are more important than your immediate life; Your integrity to yourself is more important than your body; Never fear to hurt another in a just cause," and other such statements that appear to try and create a separatist or cloister-type mentality.

I was shown that code once while I was writing and said, "Well that's not my code. I never agreed to that." Thankfully the course supervisor didn't enforce that point, though most students were shown it and recommended to read it. I finished the course pretty quickly, because at that time I was still 20 yrs old and had only tried a couple drugs, compared to someone in their 40's who had decades of things to write up.

Book 7 is called the Changing Conditions in Life Course. It is all about conditions of existence in a scale as plotted and defined by Hubbard. The conditions start at the bottom with Confusion and go up, in order, through Treason, Enemy, Doubt, Liability, Non-Existence, Danger, Emergency, Normal, Affluence and Power. Each condition has a series of steps laid out for it, and students are taught that you have to do the steps in order to move up into a higher condition. Students are also taught that if you fail to assign or apply the correct condition that the laws of the universe dictate you will automatically find yourself in the next lower condition. Remember, these are put forth as guidelines for students and are considered mandates - absolutes that have to be done. It was not open for much interpretation at all.

Students have to assess what condition they are in on each of their Dynamics and work through the steps up into at least Non-Existence on something called Repairing Past Ethical Conditions (RPEC), as anything below that is considered to be a lower condition. The steps were supposed to actually physically done, not just written about. That was a contradiction in many cases though, because it was very difficult, if not impossible, to make up damage to someone who lived in another state. Making up the damage may have included needing to repay money to their employer or parents, fix damaged property or be there to read bedtime stories for their children. It is rare to be able to simply wave some magical Hubbard wand and make past conditions go away from afar, so most people find themselves pretending as if they really did make amends. After RPEC is done they then have to assess their present-time (PT) conditions and start working up from there.

Any time students were caught doing things they weren't supposed to, such as missing too many role calls, having sex with another student or breaking some other rules, they would be assigned to something called an ethics cycle. These usually consisted of having to re-study parts of Books 5, 6 and 7 and then some form of work or manual labor to make up the damage as part of their Liability formula steps. Once that was done then they had to go around and get signatures asking for students to accept them back into the group. If students repeatedly broke rules, or brought drugs on to campus, then they would be suspended for a period of time or dismissed permanently depending on the infraction.

There were students who did actual manual labor there as part of their ethics cycles, especially if they had some sort of skill or trade. There were people who helped with plumbing or construction and maintenance, clearing brush, sanding and repainting things, and other stuff such as working in the kitchen to serve food and wash dishes.

The last part of the program is Book 8 and is called The Way to Happiness Course, which is based entirely off L. Ron Hubbard's book that used 21 precepts primarily borrowed from other sources. It is supposed to be a common sense guide to better living. Most of it is very obvious stuff, like respect your elders, be truthful, don't murder, brush your teeth, etc. One part that has continually been a problem for the program is the one that says do not drink alcohol in excess.

Narconon doesn't differentiate substance abuse from addiction. They believe that everyone can be cured by applying the same Tech to their lives, with the exception of course to SPs and people continually connected to SPs. So for one person who has been sober for a number of years but had more of a behavioral issue than a physiological addiction, not drinking alcohol to excess at some time in the future would be doable. Maybe only programs such as Moderation Management would approve of continued drinking fresh out of treatment since their approach seems to be more about reduction and control. This was more of the mindset I had initially going in - to basically just get my shit together and figure out what I wanted to do in life. Boredom and lack of direction were big factors in my alcohol abuse between the ages of 18 and 21.

For many Narconon graduates they use this part to say, "Well, cocaine was my drug of choice, not alcohol, so it's okay to drink in moderation." The obvious danger in this is that when recent substance abusers start to feel the buzz from alcohol then they begin to make irrational decisions, and next thing you know they are out looking for their drug of choice again.

Then there is also the problem of the people who had a much more severe alcohol problem such as those who would be classified as being a true alcoholic. These people typically cannot drink at all because they cannot control it in the least bit and always wind up drunk. These are also people who typically have very severe withdrawal symptoms such as seizures. Looking at this severity of an issue, one might be able to see how having the precept about drinking alcohol at the very end of the Narconon program isn't exactly a safe thing to tell recent substance abusers of any level in most cases.

I never stated that I intended to remain abstinent after leaving the program. In fact, I said that I did plan on drinking after I left, but that I just wanted to find a path in life and therefore wouldn't fall back in to the same old routines. By then I had figured out that I didn't want to go to college for any particular degree, so I thought I really needed to find something else to work toward and be a part of.

I can say that I enjoyed my time as a student at Narconon. It was more like some kind of alternative high school. Despite the varied ages and backgrounds, little cliques would develop and I made friends. After class one night almost every week I got to go into town with one another student and a couple staff members to play tennis. On weekends we'd go to the community pool in town or play basketball. We played cards a lot, smoked a ton of cigarettes and mostly just hung out. It really wasn't at all like an actual treatment center. As I mentioned before, it is mostly the fellow students who help each other while there, and also the main reason that many people report enjoying their time as a student at Narconon - it isn't because of the program, but because of the relationships developed.

My parents came out for my graduation of the program. I had a very tearful but short speech. I was sorry for causing any pain, harm, embarrassment or inconvenience to my parents. I was recruited to stay for staff but wasn't ready to commit to something like that yet as I was still only 20 yrs old, but at the same time I was going to miss many of the friends that I had made while there.

The next day I flew out of Wichita and my parents drove to see friends in another part of Kansas and flew out of Kansas City a day later. When I got on the plane there was a young flight attendant who was flirty and wearing one of the pilot's jackets to keep warm before taking off. Shortly afterward she asked me if I wanted a beer. I told her no thanks. Then she offered again and I told her I didn't have any money. She said she'd give me one, so I said that I was underage, but that still wasn't a deterrent for her. She said she wouldn't tell anyone. I then told her that I had just gotten out of a rehab program, to which her reply was, "So do you want a beer, or not?" I finally accepted.

When I got off the plane my brother picked me up. My friends had a party for my return and I got drunk that night. I was ashamed, but still had it in my head that I was going to turn my life around. I just wasn't sure how yet.

I wound up getting a job at a bar that we used to hang out at before, which wasn't smart. During this time I continued to drink pretty heavily most nights and even wound up taking ecstasy a few times. I eventually moved down to Tampa and Palm Harbor, FL late the next spring with my roommate where things continued to get worse for me. He got arrested for a DUI and I lost any desire to work after waiting tables at two other restaurants. I had gotten very depressed, and in an ecstasy- and alcohol-fueled bout of frustration I contemplated taking my own life. My roommate had a handgun, but the thing that stopped me was that I knew that I didn't want to die and I didn't want to cause any more pain or harm for others, especially my family. I just wasn't sure where I belonged in the world.

I was 21 and still lost. I had started accumulating debt and remembered that I had some military recruiters calling me after I first left college who offered me a $20,000 signing bonus. I thought that I could go into the Army for three years, get my debt paid off and come out with some money in my pocket to start over. I called my brother, who was a former Military Policeman in the Marines to get his advice, but he knew that wasn't something that I really wanted to do. I called my parents and they could tell I was feeling desperate and asked me if I thought I should go back to Narconon, and I said yes.

Within a week I was sitting in Home 5 at Narconon Chilocco playing cards and hanging out again. It was a year later, but there were quite a few familiar faces. Many of the staff members were still there, some had started working there who were students before and some were back doing the program again like me. We were called retreads.

Something was a little different though. I was a year older and I remember being more determined to do something with my life and be a responsible adult. I started moving through the retread program quickly. When I was in the sauna I was running a lot and I seemed energized. We also had almost daily volleyball games, with tournaments on the weekends. I found myself waking up very early and writing again. I began to not only grow up more, but I also became more aware of my senses. I was much more perceptive again, which I had been as a child and somehow tried to forget.

I was also reading a lot. My favorites were the Conversations with God series by Neale Donald Walsch. They seemed to make a lot of sense to me. I also read two books by Dan Millman and I began to feel much more alive over all. These feelings of invigoration weren't really because of Narconon, they were almost in spite of it. Although I attributed much of it to the program at the time, being in an environment where I didn't have to worry about outside influences and responsibilities was a big factor. I could spend a lot of time examining life while also having artistic and athletic drives and hanging out with friends. All of those things were much more of a factor for me.

One day I was at breakfast and a girl named Amy sat down in front of me. She had gone out to a place in Sacramento called HealthMed to do the sauna program that supposedly had more medical supervision because of her medication history. People who had taken certain psychiatric drugs for longer periods of time were considered to be heavier risks.

I felt an instant connection with Amy, like I could read her thoughts. It was deep and unexplainable, as well as mutual. Over the next few weeks we spent a lot of time together and decided that we would like to try and have a relationship when we left. Usually this is a big no-no to try and hook up with someone you meet at a treatment center. She was from Louisiana and was going to come to Georgia to live with me.

I finished my retread program in early September of 1999 and started to work at one of my parents' dental offices as an administrative assistant. Amy finished a couple weeks later and I picked her up at the end of the month.

After she found a job and her parents helped her get a car, we eventually found an apartment together and tried to make it work.

3 BECOMING A SCIENTOLOGIST

After my experience at Narconon the second time I decided I was going to read a bunch of Scientology books. I read every one that my parents had and bought a couple more. As part of my compensation, my dad took $5,000 out of my salary for the year and purchased four intensives (12 1/2 hours each) of introductory auditing from Mary Rieser for me. I agreed to work for him for a full year so that amount would be paid back. I remember being very excited about having a new job, living in a new apartment, and having 50 hours of auditing to do. That would be the least expensive auditing cost per hour I ever purchased.

There was a problem though. Amy was what Scientologists called an illegal pre-Clear (PC), which means there were one or more things that disqualified her from receiving auditing. It was something that immediately created a rift in our relationship, because here was a group and subject matter I was very interested in and they were telling me that the person I lived with was not okay for me.

Illegal PCs are usually because of some type of psychiatric treatments or therapies, such as the medications she had been taking before Narconon. While it didn't fully make sense, I bought into it and it was a big contributing factor to the breakdown of our relationship. It made her feel less, and made me feel like I was somehow better, a highly judgmental view that is a continuing theme espoused by Hubbard. Scientologists love to judge others, because they feel they are the only ones who really know about life and everyone else is just playing their game.

One night Amy and I went out to dinner, and then decided to have a drink. We went to a bar and had one drink. It never went beyond social drinking for me, though it did become somewhat regular again. I was told by Mary that I needed to do something called the PTS/SP Course.

So I went down to the church in Atlanta (the Org, as it's called) to get started on the course, but before I could start it I had to watch a film called Orientation. The script was written by Hubbard and it gave an overview of what happens at a church of Scientology. It starred a Scientologist actor named Larry Anderson (who is no longer a member). Toward the end of the film Anderson said, "If you leave this room after seeing this film, and walk out and never mention Scientology again, you can do so. It would be stupid, but you can do it. You can also dive off a bridge or blow your brains out. That is your choice. But, if you don't walk out that way, if you continue with Scientology, we will be very happy with you and you will be very happy with you. You will have proven that you are a friend of yours."

Again, a huge indicator to turn around and run, but instead was just something was mentally written off.

When I got onto the PTS/SP Course, I saw that it was a heavily-expanded version of Book 5 at Narconon. It included the same drills of the 12 social and anti-social characteristics, and much more.

Scientologists may claim to be against labeling people, as in psychiatric diagnoses and labels, yet they are highly guilty of doing the same thing themselves. PTS and SP are thrown around continuously, as are many other terms and acronyms that are equally ridiculous. It would be used like this:

"What's up with Tom?"

"Oh, he's PTS because his brother is a Christian and keeps telling him Scientology is bad."

Just like that, it throws a dagger in the middle of human fabric, all because Hubbard wanted to keep his flock close and lashed out at people who were critical of his creation. This sentiment has only been amplified since then.

Needless to say, my relationship with Amy didn't last much longer. This was another major sign that Scientology was going to continue to have a negative impact on my life. It even got to the point in one of my auditing sessions that I had conjured up the idea, with the encouragement of Mary through indicating with the e-meter, that I had known Amy in one or more past lifetimes and that she preyed on me then and was always someone who wasn't good for me. The weird indications from dream-like fabrications that were "validated" by the e-meter continued throughout my involvement, becoming more delusional the deeper I got.

Hubbard created what he called the Bridge to Total Freedom. It is a series of steps that are supposed to climb higher and higher to spiritual enlightenment and super-human abilities. The current highest level is called OT VIII. OT stands for Operating Thetan, as in a spiritual being who is not confined to just earthly things.

At OT VIII, one is supposed to be cause over life, and the name for that level is called Truth Revealed. I have met quite a few people who completed up through OT VIII. Some were great people and appeared to be successful and happy, while others seemed very unhappy and less capable than people who never tried Scientology. You're also supposed to be more or less free from illnesses and diseases at OT VIII, yet I personally knew of at least two women who got breast cancer after reaching that level and had to have mastectomies. I also knew of two others who were frequently sick and had to go back for more "touch-ups".

Anyway, back to the Bridge. The Narconon program is made up of several lower-level introductory Scientology courses, including three that are officially part of this Bridge. These are the Training Routines (TRs), Purification Rundown (called the New Life Detoxification Program at Narconon) and the Objectives processes.

Since I had completed those at Narconon, I could start with Mary at the next level on the Bridge. This is true for all people who go to Narconon and wind up doing more Scientology, yet Narconon claims to not be Scientology. There is also the fact that Narconon graduates use more Scientology terms than your average beginning Scientologist.

While doing my auditing with Mary and the course at the Org, I had decided that I wanted to work for Narconon. I had heard that they were going to be getting a new facility, and I was offered the position to do drug education, which included training in Boston for a couple of months prior to going back out to Oklahoma. By then it had been a year since I finished my retread and I had proven to myself that I could live in the outside world, but the idea of doing something new and being back with a familiar group was exciting to me.

4 JOININ STAFF AT NARCONON

In September of 2000, I packed up my things and started driving north to New England to train with Bobby Wiggins, the guy who developed Narconon's current drug education and prevention program. I was also going to be filling in for him while he traveled. Ironically, the first place I was staying was with Marie Cecchini, who had married George Veliskakis. They were living in New Hampshire and she had become the Executive Director of Narconon Boston, which only did the drug education.

I arrived on a weekend and Marie showed me how to get to the office, which then was just outside of Boston in Everett, MA. That is when I met Bobby Wiggins for the first time. He was developing a training course for the Narconon drug prevention specialist based on the hundreds of thousands of kids he had given presentations to. He had done some training with other Narconon staff around the world, but I was going to be the first fully-apprenticed person on this course. He had just received a Freedom Medal award from the International Association of Scientologists (IAS) the previous year and Narconon was a hot item in the Scientology world at that time.

Bobby's entire series of lectures are based on books and other references written by L. Ron Hubbard. He developed stories and some good hooks or angles to keep the kids interesting and having fun, but the core information is all straight from Hubbard and designed to create a favorable opinion of him with subtle indoctrination early on in life.

Some of the Hubbard principles given to students in these prevention lectures include talking about the "time track" and mental image pictures, the sauna detoxification program from Clear Body, Clear Mind, Study Tech, the Tone Scale of emotions and much more.

The first few things he had me do is to read the applicable references from L. Ron Hubbard, including definitions out of the Dianetics and Scientology Technical Dictionary.

On the Narconon Drug Education Lecture Hat (job description) given to me in September of 2000, the Hubbard references are as follows:

Clear Body, Clear Mind by L. Ron Hubbard
Dianetics 55 by L. Ron Hubbard

From the Hubbard Communications Office Bulletins (HCOBs)

HCOB 28 Aug 68 II	"Drugs"
HCOB 29 Aug 68	"Drug Data"
HCOB 8 Jan 69	"Drugs and Insanity"
HCOB 17 Oct 69	"Drugs, Aspirin and Tranquilizers"
HCOB 7 Aug 79	"False Data Stripping"
HCOB 25 Sep 71 RB Revised 1 Apr 78	"Tone Scale in Full"
HCOB 26 Oct 70	"Obnosis and the Tone Scale"

Definition #3 of "Time Track" in the Dianetics and Scientology Technical Dictionary

From the Hubbard Communications Office Policy Letters (HCO PLs)

Marketing Series #1-4

Then he wanted me to write down a short version of my personal story that would be used as my introduction to students after reading through the entire hat write-up.

One of the key training exercises used included standing in front of each other and saying "hello" in the various emotions listed on Hubbard's Tone Scale. This was called doing Mood Drills, and they were done over and over and over. Bobby had told me that those were also good exercises for actors to do, and that he had been a B-movie actor in his previous lifetime. He said Scientologist actors frequently did drills with the Tone Scale.

The Tone Scale itself is a list of emotions or attitudes that were arbitrarily assigned numbers ranging from -40 on the bottom for Total Failure to 40 at the top for Serenity of Beingness. Right in the middle is Body Death at 0.0. The numbers are not linear, as some have decimals and others skip over larger increments. Some of the more interesting levels include Controlling Bodies, Being a Body and Owning Bodies. The church has a film that acts out all of the tone levels with people simply repeating "AEIOU" over and over again. Thankfully, we just drilled the ones above Body Death! Believe me, the insanity of all of this is not lost on me now, and learning to laugh at myself has been extremely therapeutic since then.

The next things on the training and apprenticeship program were to practice my introduction over and over again until I could go through it comfortably, followed by practicing each of the presentations themselves. I found myself feeling like I needed to embellish my personal story to make the details seem more harrowing and my drug problem more extensive than it was - that somehow this would give me more "street credit" with the students and my presentations more interesting. In actuality, I could have kept my talks to just about what can happen when you drink too much in high school and college.

My first live presentation was to a small high school class in Stoneham, MA where the teacher and students were tolerant of my novice attempt. I definitely messed up and embarrassed myself, but it wound up being ok overall, and from then on I was practically set. It was sort of like hitting off the first tee in a round of golf with spectators.

I'd go out to the schools with Bobby and sometimes we would split up the presentations, or he would do some and I would do some. This continued throughout the rest of September and early into October, and by that time I had gotten comfortable enough to do all of the presentations on my own, which would include some for kids in early elementary school all the way up through high school. Bobby and I spent many hours talking, drinking coffee from Dunkin' Donuts and smoking cigarettes.

Then later that month Bobby went over to England for the annual IAS event, which he was required to be present for since he was a Freedom Medal winner. That event featured the announcement of Narconon Chilocco moving to the new Arrowhead facility, which was purchased and renovated with IAS funds, to the tune of about $3.5 million. After that event Bobby went out to Oklahoma to do a bit of training with some students and staff before finally returning back to Boston. He also delivered presentations in Oklahoma to local schools near the area of the new facility as a goodwill mission and PR effort. It was during Red Ribbon Week, which is the national drug prevention week. I covered his presentations in New England and spoke to 5,000 students that week, criss-crossing Massachusetts, New Hampshire, Vermont, Connecticut and Maine.

When he returned it was time for the local church in Boston to show the video from the IAS event. I had never been to an IAS event before. They are actually nothing more than internal propaganda events used to keep the Scientologist flock in line and to continue extracting as much money as possible from parishioners.

At that big event Bobby had me stand up in front of everyone after it was over and told them about my being a Narconon graduate, having trained with him for drug prevention and that I was getting ready to go out to the new Arrowhead facility to be in charge of its drug education department. IAS fundraisers, both Sea Org staff and people like Bobby, get inside information on the financial situation of church members. They find out things such as how much money they make, what kind of cars they drive, where they live and how much their homes cost, etc. to get an idea of who they can really target for larger amounts of money. That night there was a younger guy who was a computer programmer of some type and Bobby put him on the spot to pay nearly $3,000 to get an IAS Lifetime membership for me.

I felt oddly indebted since I didn't know much about the IAS. I was excited about the new facility but also humbled by being put on display and exploited for money. I got caught up in the hoopla and mixture of emotions and left feeling rather important. Self-importance, status issues and judgmental views of others turned out to be a common theme among Scientologists. It's all about where you are, who's on top, what you've done and how much money you have given.

The IAS is supposed to raise money for the advancement and protection of Scientology, and claims to give grants to Scientology-related activities, such as the Narconon Arrowhead building. However, much later I came to find out it was something very different. Back then, though, I thought it was cool to be part of it all. I bought into the idea that I was on this incredibly important team that was dedicated to saving the planet for the good of all mankind.

On the weekends Bobby would go around to various IAS fundraising events and give "briefings" about the state of things in Scientology land in order to get even more money, and he would be paid a commission from everything collected at these other smaller events.

One time I rode in the car with him and an IAS staff member in the Sea Org named Annie to go around and do surprise visits to people with money who were not confirmed for the event in their town that evening. I remember hearing Annie talk about how "flush" one guy was and that he needed to "cough up at least two G's". This was part of the whole process, a rare early look for me at the level of extortion that runs so deep in Scientology. Staff members, especially those in the Sea Org (the ones who sign the billion-year contracts to serve Scientology for many lifetimes), typically believe that they are doing their part by dedicating their lives to Scientology, and so people who have nice things and regular jobs on the outside are thought to have less purpose and therefore owe lots of money to the cause.

At the beginning of November two guys arrived in Boston from Oklahoma to train and replace me in the work I was doing there - Steve and Justin. Bobby and I began training them, and I would often take both of them with me by myself to present to schools when Bobby was out of town doing other things.

Marie had gotten frustrated that I demanded full pay (since I was performing all of the income-producing activities at that time) and suddenly said I should be paying her rent. Well that was never part of my agreement for being up there, so I moved out of her house and wound up getting a hotel room at the Red Roof Inn on the border of Massachusetts and New Hampshire. It was $350 per week to rent the room and I paid for the first week, but was only making $330 per week at the time, and Justin and Steve were staying with me. A couple nights Bobby also stayed there, as he no longer had a place to live in Boston, and Justin was able to pay for a few nights on his credit card.

Steve decided he wanted to stay with Marie instead of trying to pitch in for the room, and had gotten keys to a spare car that someone from the Boston Org had loaned to Narconon. He was supposed to meet us at a school one morning but never showed up. He had taken some cash he was given for gas money and bought some Klonopin off the street and relapsed. He wound up leaving that night to go back home.

There was another IAS event while I was up there that was held in New York City in early November also. I drove down from Boston to Connecticut with Justin. We met Bobby at his hotel room and then the three of us rode into NYC together. It was my first time there. We got there in time to tour the Scientology church just off Times Square, which also was home to several East US Sea Org offices.

The event itself was held in a banquet room of a restaurant a couple blocks away. It started off with a short video showing all of Bobby's accomplishments and when he was presented with his Freedom Medal. Then he got in front of everyone with a microphone and started the enthusiastic process of fleecing members while Annie worked the room. I got excited about the event and wound up giving all of the cash I had in my pocket that night (about $110), and Justin gave $450 on a credit card for an annual membership. It was easy to get caught up in the excitement when Narconon was such a featured item at these fundraising events.

Soon after the event Justin wound up leaving to handle

something with family, but he never came back. I later found out that he had also relapsed. I couldn't afford to stay in the hotel anymore, and wasn't going to Marie's house again, so I decided to sleep in the office. The bathroom there had a shower, and I had a pillow and blanket in my car. It turned out that the shower had no hot water.

I spent the next three weeks sleeping on the floor in the office and taking cold showers so I could save up a few hundred dollars. This included spending my birthday and Thanksgiving alone. I finally had enough and informed them I would be leaving the first week of December. Marie and the other administrative staff member, Lisbeth (from Denmark), tried to keep me there longer and even wrote reports on me for trying to leave, but I had already been there three months and was only supposed to be there for two. They said I was responsible for finding a replacement for myself, but that was never part of the deal – Bobby was the one who needed to find a replacement for his self since the original plan was for me to go to Oklahoma.

On Friday, December 1, 2000, I got my last paycheck from Narconon Boston at 3:50 PM and was able to walk next door to the bank and get it cashed before it closed at 4:00 PM. I then said my goodbyes, got a last cup of coffee from the Dunkin' Donuts that was frequented, and hit the road. I had a map and was pointed southwest toward Oklahoma, ready to drive as far as possible that night, which wound up being a snowy rest stop in the West Virginia hills around 3 AM.

Arriving Back in Oklahoma

I arrived at Narconon Chilocco in Oklahoma at 1 AM on Sunday, December 3rd, and was given a temporary room at Home 5 again until I could get officially signed up for staff. Since I had completed the training and internship in Boston, I didn't have to do the regular training program in Oklahoma as long as I finished my basic staff courses within a certain period of time.

I was eager to get to work every day. I would arrive around

7:30 AM and would often work until 10:30 PM. I was making roughly $250 per week, before taxes, to do so. It was exciting for me. I felt like I belonged. I was young and thought that I was doing something good for the world - at least that was my intention.

In Boston the services are supported through grants and donations as well as the schools paying for the presentations, so the first thing I wanted to do was send out some fundraising letters. I wound up printing them asking for donations from WISE companies throughout the country. I sent out about 3,000 letters and got back roughly $1,600 in funding. I also researched businesses and foundations in Oklahoma and sent letters to them as well over the next few months and wound up getting maybe the same amount again. In all, it wasn't very much money to fund the activity, and the schools weren't going to pay, so it was looked at as a PR activity funded by the facility.

I found myself having a hard time just getting a school to say yes to a free presentation at first. There were people doing work down in McAlester, near where the new facility was going to be located and so I was able to give a couple presentations there. With each school, we would give them a letter stating that someone gave money to sponsor their school and that it would be great if they could write something back to them afterward to explain what their thoughts were. A short, three-question survey was also left for the students to give feedback in their own words and often times teachers would send them back to us with the letters. I loved talking to the kids and the teachers, and quite frankly didn't fully realize at the time how much crap was in those lectures. I was becoming more and more of a True Believer Scientologist, and it was beginning to overtake my general good will toward others as being the highest purpose for doing things.

While I was working on getting things set up more, I found myself in the position of training two more people. One guy was Joshua Bencke, who was the first paid trainee to do the Narconon Drug Prevention Specialist course in Oklahoma. He wound up setting up the short-lived Narconon Rio Grande education office outside Albuquerque, NM. He had gotten a large grant from a local company to fund his activities, although I don't believe he stayed in operation more than a couple years and went on to do something else.

The other person I was training was a local guy from Oklahoma named Bobby Newman. He was a good guy who meant well and never had any experience in anything like this since his prior profession was a sheet metal worker. He definitely wanted to help and had strong intention to learn things like typing, working with a computer, making calls to schools and doing other administrative work.

I took Joshua and Bobby with me frequently on presentations, and at other times I would have them in the office calling schools while I went out for the talks. They both had to learn all the various duties in running a fully-functional operation - to wear all of the hats. Throughout the winter and spring we were able to start to fill in more days on the calendar before the school year ended, because we used each letter we got back from a school presentation to book new schools, and with each new school who said yes there was usually a neighboring school that would also allow us to speak.

When we would travel down to McAlester we were able to stay in one of the cabins around the lake while work was being done on the main facility. There was mounting excitement about the move. Joshua eventually finished his training and was ready to head back to New Mexico, and Bobby and I continued spending a lot of time together. I started telling him more about my experience with Scientology and how I had completed something called the Drug Rundown with Mary in Georgia before joining staff. I encouraged Bobby to get some auditing, as well did Derry Hallmark, who also became good friends with him. Derry was a senior executive there and was one of the people who was involved in recruiting me for staff as well.

One day while driving down to the new facility, Bobby and I were talking about Scientology and Narconon. He had a couple auditing sessions with Mary by then that he had purchased when she came out to audit other staff. I shared with him that day what others had shared with me previously - the best EP (end phenomena) of the Narconon program was not just for people to stop doing drugs, but to have a desire to go up the Bridge in

Scientology.

"Don't you think that's at least a bit deceiving?" Bobby asked. His point was right on the mark, as anyone who hadn't been brainwashed yet could see.

My reply was, "Well, it's like an undercut to a church. They're not at a point of realizing they need Scientology yet, so this way they are getting some Scientology and now have an opportunity to reach for all of it. Those who stay off drugs but don't join the church are great, but the ones who do move up the Bridge are the best products that Narconon has. It's the greatest good."

Yes, I had definitely become a True Believer at that point. In time, so would he.

My Sea Org Recruitment

Several Scientologist auditors would frequent Narconon Chilocco to provide auditing services to staff members there who paid for it. As I mentioned, Mary Rieser was one of them, and since I still had prepaid hours left with her I was able to continue going in session with her. Around May of 2001 something interesting happened while I was in an auditing session. I believed I had already been involved in Dianetics and Scientology in my previous lifetime, and that I thought I had already reached the state of Clear (more on past-life stuff later). This was then further "validated" by the reaction on the e-meter.

The standard protocol in such a case is to have the person go to one of the upper churches and do something called a Clear Certainty Rundown (CCRD), which is supposed to verify whether or not someone had in fact achieved this state of Clear that Hubbard invented. It is supposed to be a person who has gotten rid of his "reactive mind", which is what Hubbard thought of as being a continual collection of past trauma filled with pain and suffering that had a stimulus-response effect on people. He theorized in Dianetics that a person who no longer has his reactive mind and is Clear has near-perfect memory and mental ability and is virtually impervious to illness and disease. This particular state proved to be one of the most difficult things for him and all of Scientology, it seemed, and wound up becoming an integral part of my departure as well in the future.

However, back in 2001 my auditing folders were sent to the Advanced Organization Los Angeles (AOLA) to do the CCRD. I wound up staying in a rented room of a Scientologist's apartment a few blocks away and would walk down every morning that week to L. Ron Hubbard Blvd, which is home to Pacific Area Command (PAC) for Scientology and includes several Scientology organizations, buildings and offices. It is also the spot of the famous "Big Blue" building with the Scientology sign at the top where many members of the Sea Org live.

Sea Org members began working with Hubbard literally at sea on his boats and were the beginning of his para-military group that he commanded. They sign billion-year contracts in devotion to him and the cause, and now staff up higher level organizations throughout the world. There are roughly about 20,000 Sea Org members or so today, though there are many more who have joined and then left.

One day I was getting coffee at the canteen below one of the buildings and was approached by another young man who was wearing a regular suit instead of a Sea Org uniform. His name was Brandon and he kept eyeballing me before finally approaching.

He was short and had dark, slicked-back hair. His smile was something that sticks with me to this day as a characteristic of many Scientologists I met over time - one that indicated he knew something I didn't and was therefore better than me in some way.

After basic introductions and finding out why I was there, etc. he started in with this really secretive-sounding sales pitch. He was a Sea Org recruiter, specifically for Bridge Publications. Bridge Publications is a separate company, but is only staffed by Sea Org members and only publishes things for Dianetics and Scientology. He wanted me to come by his office and get a much more detailed "briefing" on the state of the world and how I could help. I told him I was already helping by working at Narconon, but he started the covert invalidation disguised as flattery by saying I should be doing something more important.

After initially saying I wasn't interested, I finally agreed to meet up with him the next day. After all, I was curious about this "special briefing" he had, since I naturally think there are deeper meanings to most situations and events in life and thought maybe I could find out something new. That is their hook - the curiosity about the unknown.

The next day Brandon met me at a coffee house a couple of blocks away with his fellow recruiter, Blake. In contrast to Brandon, Blake was tall and his smile seemed much more inviting and genuine. We sat outside and initially talked about all of the basic questions I had about joining the Sea Org, such as where I would live, what I would do, etc. I also wanted to know about relationships. Blake told me he had a "smokin' hot" wife and that there were plenty of girls in the Sea Org. He said he could introduce me to many of his wife's friends after I joined.

Brandon and Blake put on a pretty convincing show. They wanted me to work with them specifically at Bridge Publications, which actually paid minimum wage (rather than the $50 per week most Sea Org members get paid) and where you weren't required to wear a uniform. Although they were paid more, their room and board was deducted from their pay and they also were responsible for their own clothes. Blake even had a car and on the outside they seemed to have a relatively normal life. They made me feel really wanted, which was another attraction. Clearly I had a pattern of feeling like I needed to belong to something.

Later that afternoon I went into their office and sat down to watch a Sea Org recruitment video, which included interviews with lots of attractive, smiling faces doing all kinds of jobs in apparently one big, happy family-type atmosphere to save the planet. While still a bit intriguing, the cheese factor, like virtually all of Scientology's films, was undeniable.

Soon after the film was over came time for the interesting part of the briefing. They had a special large binder full of articles, clips, quotes and examples. The whole thing outlined how an elite group of people were really in control over much of planet Earth and that their plans are moving further along and we are getting closer to total destruction. It highlighted Hubbard's writings about how incredibly important he was and that his brainchildren were the only ones who could save mankind and thus the planet.

After that came the heavy sales pitch - they told me I was a "big being" and that the only way I could really live up to my full potential was to be in the Sea Org and that there was no greater purpose in life than to be part of "the most ethical group on the planet". Anything or anyone saying otherwise was just "CI" (counter-intention) or the reactive bank agreeing with societal decay. In other words, it was a huge guilt trip that I would be letting the whole world down if I didn't do it.

I told them I would think about it and get back to them after I was done with my CCRD, which was the whole reason I was in LA. Turns out that I was told there wasn't enough evidence of being Clear and that I should continue on with my auditing until something further is uncovered or happens. During the next couple of days Brandon and Blake courted me heavily, introducing me to a few pretty women in the Sea Org close to my age, taking me out to lunch, driving around to see other parts of Los Angeles, and generally trying to make me feel very welcome.

I eventually agreed that I would do it, and went along with their plan and signed the billion-year contract. I began routing in up to just before the point where I would have started what is called the Estates Project Force (EPF), which is basically Sea Org boot camp. In order to do that, there were several things that had to be taken care of. First, I had to talk to my parents and take care of some debts. I had bought a car from them and owed them money for it, so Brandon and Blake wanted me to get them to forgive the debt so I could keep the car or just sell the car and give them the money. They were not immediately agreeable and said I couldn't just take the car and wanted me to think things over more, but they said they would respect my decision.

I also had to call the Executive Director of Narconon Chilocco, Gary Smith, because I was supposed to find a replacement for my position there. Gary said he was fine with it, but that he wanted me to help with the move to the new facility at Arrowhead and that after the grand opening and I trained a replacement for myself, that he would allow me to break the five-year contract that I had with Narconon to join the Sea Org.

I was put on what was called a project prepare, meaning that I had agreed to join but needed to handle a few things first, but was started on the official routing form to begin. The first thing needed was approval, so I answered a very thorough life history questionnaire, which asked about every possible area of your life including sexual relations, drug use, criminal activity, family history, health, goals, and more. After that I sat and did an interview with someone who read over my life history and asked more details while I was on the e-meter, checking to see if I had left anything out or tried to downplay any negative aspects. After this deep, embarrassing and sometimes painful probing of my past, I was eventually given the green light to continue on with the routing form.

Blake and Brandon walked me around to various people to get them to sign off their portions of the form, and by that night, we got to the person who was in charge of the EPF, where I was supposed to be officially welcomed into the Sea Org. Fittingly, we were standing under a big banner that carried the Sea Org motto "We Come Back", as I was there believing that I had been involved in Scientology before this lifetime. This woman looked at me, asked what was going on, Brandon answered for me and she completed the initiation, indicating that my next step on the form was to report to the person in charge of new arrivals.

Thankfully, I never got any further on that routing form and caught my plane the next morning back to Oklahoma.

Moving from Chilocco to Arrowhead

When I returned from Los Angeles we were in full transition mode from Chilocco to Arrowhead. There were Sea Org members at the new Arrowhead facility running the final renovations from the Church of Scientology International Landlord's Office. They wanted the facility to look perfect for the showcase grand opening, which was scheduled for later that summer.

In preparation for the move, there was an entire PR plan that had been running about a year before the move actually took place. This involved two full-time staff members attending community events and spreading money around the Lake Eufaula area in towns such as Canadian, Crowder, Eufaula and McAlester. Vicki Smith and Peggy Bunda schmoozed with legislators, senior centers, chambers of commerce, churches and other organizations to gain good favor ahead of time.

Despite all of the fears of Scientology locally, enough air cover was bought off. One of the key people at the time was Oklahoma State Senator Gene Stipe, who had held a seat in office for roughly 50 consecutive years and was the go-to guy in the area to get things done. Stipe was sold on the economic impact of having a facility that size in his locale, including hiring local people and millions in new spending for Pittsburg and McIntosh Counties. Stipe's legacy was later disgraced when he was prosecuted for campaign fraud and put on house arrest. Even Gene Stipe Blvd was renamed after his indictment. His constituents were very polarized; some thought he was one of the greatest men to ever live there while others thought he was one of the biggest crooks. Like many career politicians, both could have been true.

When it came time for the move itself, 99 students and 99 staff all went from north-central Oklahoma to the southeastern part primarily in one large caravan. Only a skeleton crew remained back at Chilocco to continue cleaning out the remaining belongings and ensuring the property was in satisfactory condition when it was turned back over to the Five Civilized Tribes who had leased the property to Narconon.

While the move took place in late July, the grand opening was slated for the next month. A budget of roughly $100,000 was set aside for the event and even more was spent. Staff from ABLE International, as well as volunteers from around the country, were flown in to help with the planning and preparation. ABLE stands for the Association for Better Living and Education, and is the branch of Scientology that controls the church's social betterment groups. It is staffed entirely by Sea Org members.

By then I had already started to make a bit of a name for myself internally since I was the main drug education person, had high testing scores, began writing articles and press releases for distribution, and had even started helping on websites and doing radio interviews. I had been promoted to work with the Senior

Director of Expansion, Derry Hallmark, and help him oversee three divisions.

I was sort of pushed into helping with the grand opening, mainly since Derry didn't want to have anything to do with it. I was assigned the lowly task of heading up the tours of the facility after the ribbon was cut. We had to organize a route through the facility and I had a series of staff members posted throughout the building to explain their various job functions and portions of the program to the people who were coming in.

Students were either allowed to attend or stay in their rooms. They were not allowed to just roam around the facility. Those who did attend wore special shirts indicating them and had to sign confidentiality waivers since they would be viewed by the general public and possibly be included in video and still photography.

A special message was recorded on camera by Kirstie Alley and played on a loop, since she was still technically the official celebrity spokesperson at the time. She had promised to come down and have a big party, but she never showed up.

The grand opening itself was headed up by Rena Weinberg, President of ABLE International, and Clark Carr, President of Narconon International and Gary Smith. It was also supposed to be the introduction of Arrowhead's newly-appointed President, Michael Anzalone. Michael had just finished up going through lower conditions and making amends for having inappropriate contact with a local district attorney earlier that year.

In addition to the ABLE staff and multiple volunteers, a few Scientologists were hired to professionally produce the event. There was also a video crew from Golden Era Productions, which is Scientology's internal audio/visual production team. The grand opening was to be featured in upcoming Scientology events.

The speakers and presenters included State Senator Gene Stipe, White House Director of Faith and Community-Based Treatment Clifton Mitchell, local mayors, Gary Smith, Michael Anzalone, Rena Weinberg and Clark Carr. It was quite the production, to say the least, and with all of the church staff members on hand it was always a push for the PR of it all, with less focus on the actual care for the students. Confidentiality laws and treatment schedules became secondary to the production of the grand opening. The majority of the staff and students were highly ticked off as a result.

During this whole time Rena Weinberg took an interest in me for some reason. She found out that I had signed a Sea Org contract with Bridge Publications and said that if I was going to join them that I needed to be an ABLE staff member. She had their director of recruitment meet with me to conduct a qualifications interview at a hotel in McAlester after the grand opening, and he determined that I wasn't actually qualified for ABLE International level staff due to my history, though I might be eligible for a lower-level Sea Org position to start with. I wound up feeling a bit disappointed, but also relieved because it became a way out of joining.

Following the grand opening, two Scientologists took some of the interview footage and wound up creating a 21-minute promotional video as well as a series of radio and television public service announcements (PSAs). These PSAs were then heavily utilized to start promoting Narconon Arrowhead, and since it is listed as a 501(c)3 non-profit, we started to get some air time for free. TV and radio stations typically have a certain amount of PSA time they are either required to fill or receive tax benefits for providing each year.

Tom Cruise's First Visit to Arrowhead

In September of 2001 we had an unexpected guest. Tom Cruise flew into McAlester and caused quite a stir. He was accompanied by Penelope Cruz and Vice President of the Church of Scientology Celebrity Centre International (CC Int) Tommy Davis to tour the facility for someone who needed help. McAlester's two largest employers are a maximum security prison called Big Mac and an army ammunition plant. That plant wound up being the primary supplier of bombs used in the infamous Shock and Awe campaign, but that night in Sept. Cruise's plane flew low over the plant after having initially mistaken it for the small airport nearby. Someone from the plant called the FBI, and an agent was dispatched to Arrowhead to find out whose plane it was and why it was there.

When Cruise and Cruz toured the facility, all the students were ushered either outside or in their rooms and several staff were posted as guards throughout the facility. It was one of many examples of Scientologists getting special treatment at the facility, especially involving the Celebrity Centre. This was the first time I would come face-to-face with Cruise, but I had first mistaken Tommy Davis as him since they have similar features and Cruise was walking behind him with a baseball hat pulled down low and Penelope right behind him. I remember both of them being much smaller in stature than I had pictured.

After the tour the party met up in the President's office, which is an open second story balcony that overlooks the entire main lobby area. A Hispanic family that lived and worked at Arrowhead was brought in to help speak with Penelope and her guest, and she was kind enough to pose for a picture with them.

The fall of 2001 started to show some pretty substantial growth for Narconon Arrowhead with the advent of the PSAs, the promotion of the new facility, and riding a wave of some talented and enthusiastic staff members. It was also around during a several-year period where Narconon centers dominated much of the internet search engine space through both paid advertising as well as organic listings and their network of referral agents.

In November Anzalone was kicked off staff for having sexual relations with a female trainee, which was a direct violation of the rules. This left a vacancy for the position of president and both Clark and Rena were pushing Gary Smith to find a replacement. There were multiple examples of staff members having sex with trainees, and sometimes even with students. There were also many times where trainees would have sex with students. Any time it involved a student, the trainee or staff member was fired, to my recollection, though never reported to authorities. Of course there were also continual occurrences where students would have sex with other students, despite having full-time security and even cameras in the hallways. They were always able to get around the system and were only caught occasionally. The fact that the President of the organization had engaged in activity with a trainee was really only par for the course.

As for the newly-vacant position, I started filling in on some public relations actions such as hosting dignitaries and doing more community work. I was being considered for the job permanently and had to go through another life history questionnaire as well as state my intentions. I wound up being officially chosen for the job in December of 2001, having turned 24 just a couple weeks earlier.

5 BECOMING PRESIDENT OF ARROWHEAD

As president of Narconon Arrowhead, my duties were primarily external, meaning public relations, government relations, and other spokesperson activities. Since Arrowhead was the showcase facility I would have to host domestic and foreign dignitaries who were coming to view the program, act as sort of an ambassador to other Narconon centers, and was sort of an unofficial spokesperson for Narconon in the United States since Clark Carr spent most of his time and attention working on things in other countries.

Other duties for me at the time included being a voting member of the Executive Council for Narconon Arrowhead, which are the senior level people essentially in charge of the operations of their respective areas or divisions.

Not only is the Narconon program based wholly on materials from L. Ron Hubbard, but the organizational, management and financial directives are as well. The two sides are called the Tech (for technical delivery and application) and Admin (for the administration). Hubbard's work is often called the Tech by Scientologists as a summation of all of his collective works.

As a reward for Gary Smith, the Executive Council had decided to pay for Gary Smith to go to Flag to get some auditing. He stayed several weeks and finished both OT IV and OT V. Narconon Arrowhead paid out tens of thousands of dollars directly to Flag for that trip alone.

In Executive Council, the players were Gary Smith as the head of the organization and corporation, myself as president and spokesperson, Derry Hallmark as the Senior Director of Expansion, Kathy Gosselin as the Senior Director of Production, Michael Gosselin as the Senior Director of Administration and Deputy Executive Director and Michael St. Amand as the Director of Legal Affairs. All were long-time Scientologists, with the exception of Derry at the time, who had just been introduced to Scientology a few years earlier through Narconon.

Any time there was a disagreement, of which there were many loud ones on the Council, the deciding factor would always be to consult an L. Ron Hubbard policy. Hubbard is known as Source to Scientologists, and they're taught to always find a solution with Source material. It's like Christians asking "what would Jesus do?" but Hubbard loved to write and record nearly every utterance as being important, even when things became highly contradictory within his own Policy Letters and Bulletins.

As a very odd part of my job, Gary Smith's wife Vicki was posted in my office as my assistant. However, she really did whatever she wanted and reported to her husband, found a different title that Hubbard wrote about called an Aide so she could receive higher pay, and generally annoyed the staff with the power she assumed because she was Gary's wife. I had little say-so in what she did, despite the fact that she was posted as my Aide.

One example was that she loved having coordination meetings for various things, and they would take up time and not get much accomplished. When I voiced the fact that I'd rather stick to production and only simple coordination or regularly-standing executive meetings, she insisted that I hold a weekly PR coordination committee meeting, and got her husband to enforce it on me.

One of the people who had to attend this weekly PR meeting was a girl named Erica who worked in the division responsible for promoting the program via the radio, newspaper and television. I had a couple friends who had told me about Erica saying I should ask her out. At that time I hadn't dated anyone since before I left Georgia in September of 2000, so it had been nearly a year and a half. Erica was a tall, slender young woman who was bright and determined. The appeal was easy to see in the beginning, especially since the pool of possibilities was confined to about 150 people at the time. Rarely did anyone look to start a serious relationship outside of a fellow staff member at Arrowhead because so much of our lives were focused on the organization, including working 60+ hour weeks, living on campus and primarily socializing with co-workers when not on the job. Erica and I did start dating in January of 2002.

One day we came into work and the receptionists said the phone lines were going crazy, and that people were saying they heard about us on CNN. We later found out that Erica sent a PSA to CNN in Atlanta, and wasn't aware that it was their corporate headquarters - she thought it was a local affiliate.

We wound up getting thousands of calls from PSAs on CNN and put together a plan to try and keep them going. Erica was instructed to keep tight contact with the PSA director for CNN at the time, Brian Denney, and it wound up airing for three months.

Narconon Science Advisory Board

One of my first tasks on my new position was to help organize and host a Narconon Science Advisory Board meeting at Arrowhead. Later that year, a description of the event was written in Narconon International's newsletter, which stated:

"Narconon International held a major meeting of its Science Advisory Board at Narconon Arrowhead. Despite several inches of snow and icy highways, attendees arrived from throughout the United States, including long-time members Alfonzo Paredes, M.D.; David Root, M.D.; Shelley Beckmann, Ph.D.; and Jim Barnes. Also there were friends and consultants of Narconon Arrowhead, Sandy MacNabb and Emery Johnson, M.D. (former Asst. Surgeon General U.S.), as well as Arrowhead's new Medical Director, Dr. Gerald Wooten.

"Other attendees who shared their experiences and knowledge were Dr. Allan Sosin from Narconon Southern California, the distinguished Dr. Schoenthaler from California State University Stanislaus, and with Michael Phillips from Utah, who is completing a long-term outcome study on the reduction of crime in juveniles who've completed the New Life Center Narconon program."

At the meeting Dr. Root was elected as the Chairman of the Science Advisory Board, and Gene Stipe dropped in to welcome the members before wrapping up.

Following the meeting of the Science Advisory Board at Arrowhead in early 2002, one of the first orders of importance to try to bring Narconon to the forefront of the drug rehabilitation field in the 21st century was to have an updated, formalized outcome study completed of the program results. After all, it was widely known internally that the 76% success rate Narconon claimed was bullshit. In fact, at one point even the retention rate of Arrowhead fell below 50%, meaning that more than half the people who enrolled in the program left without completing it. There was a whole series of steps written up to improve the retention rate and technical delivery before any outcome study would have even been considered.

Rena Weinberg and Clark Carr were keen on getting Thomas McLellan to be the lead author of the Narconon outcome study. They wanted something that was legitimate and wanted to get the best. McLellan is a well-known psychologist in the addiction field and is the founder of the Treatment Research Institute as well as the person who created the Addiction Severity Index (ASI). The ASI is an industry standard tool for assessment used in the treatment field. While there was a lot of talk about McLellan and there was some initial discussion with him, he ultimately backed out because he didn't want to be associated with Narconon. Turns out he made other good career moves, as he was appointed to be the Deputy Director of the Office of National Drug Control Policy (ONDCP) years later under the Obama Administration.

To this date, a formal outcome study has still never been done on the Narconon program at any center, and they continue to knowingly lie about their success rate, which is false advertising. Narconon, ABLE and the church of Scientology are fully aware that the program doesn't get the results they claim, and are thus committing fraud daily.

The ways their promoted success rates are justified are by graduate follow-up calls and completely un-scientific reporting. I used to get the weekly report of every graduate contacted each week and how they reported that they were doing. At the bottom of each report would be a percentage listed of those reporting to be clean and sober. So let's say the staff member in charge of following up with graduates calls 300 that week, but is only able to get 100 of them on the phone. Of those 100, 70 reported they were doing well, and so that was the number indicating the success rate of the graduates at the time.

This of course completely negates the other 200 that weren't contacted, many of whom were unable to be located and therefore not a good sign to begin with, let alone the fact that any reported success was usually based on un-verified statements from the graduates themselves. Many graduates of course did not want to return, so if they were getting drunk or high again they didn't necessarily want to tell Narconon about it.

When people reported not doing well, they would be pitched to come back and do a review program, like I had done. They were usually charged half-price to redo the program, and sometimes Arrowhead would make as much as $50,000 in a single week just from people doing the program for a second, third or fourth time.

The Relationship of Arrowhead, Narconon International and ABLE

Arrowhead was, and still is, in a glorified yet unenviable position regarding the Narconon network, ABLE and Scientology. Since it was paid for by Scientologists, it was expected to cooperate with the church of Scientology fully, whereas some of the smaller, more independent centers could tell people to piss off when they really wanted to.

My job meant that I had at least three conflicting viewpoints that I was in the middle of and had to appease - the role of what was needed locally in Oklahoma and internally at the facility itself, the role of being the premier facility in the Narconon network and to help do Narconon spokesperson duties, and the role of the flagship Scientology-backed drug rehabilitation facility with ABLE and the Church.

Clark and Rena held me to a much higher standard compared to the other staff, which was both unfair and yet somewhat expected considering what happened with my predecessor. Rena found out that I was dating Erica, and sexual relationships outside of marriage are simply not allowed in the Sea Org. She told me casual relations did not fit the image of what is needed for the President of Narconon Arrowhead, and that if I still planned on joining the Sea Org, I should probably not lead Erica on any longer since she was not qualified to do so for other reasons.

Here was another major influence on relationships from the church, one that would wind up being the most difficult strain from then on. I hadn't made up my mind fully at the time, as I really wanted to be a father and children aren't allowed in the Sea Org anymore. Rena's assistant, Lisa, spoke to me about this one day when I told her I wanted kids. At the time she was only about 20 years old and told me, "We've had lots of kids before in previous lifetimes. The best thing we can do for future generations is to help save this planet."

That didn't fully handle my objection, but I did feel a very strong sense of wanting to do something very meaningful for society as a whole and thought I was on the right track at the time. (Apparently the statement that Lisa parroted back to me that she had been told by other members of the Sea Org didn't work on her fully either, because I wound up seeing years later that she was no longer in the Sea Org and had a child.)

I was torn, honestly. I really liked spending time with Erica, but I loved my job and my assumed responsibility.

In early March I told her that I could no longer see her because I wanted to join the Sea Org in the future and that it wouldn't be fair to either of us. It was upsetting to both of us at the time, and really neither fully understood why some outside influence could dictate our personal relationship like that, but it would eventually become a theme.

Going to DC

In mid-March came my first trip to Washington, DC on behalf of Narconon. On my layover in Memphis, I saw our PSAs airing on the CNN airport network, another sign of growing strength that was encouraging as I was headed to the Capitol.

I was meeting Clark and Rena there, along with Erika Christensen and her mother, who were accompanied by Vice President of CC Int Greg LeClaire. Erika was fresh off her role in the award-winning film "Traffic", where she played the drug-addicted daughter of Michael Douglas - a judge who was appointed to become the Drug Czar. In a move to try and bring more relevance to drug education, DEA Administrator Asa Hutchinson invited Erika to be on the DEA's Demand Reduction Advisory Board.

It was just the kind of PR leverage that Narconon and Scientology couldn't let go to waste, because Christensen is a second-generation Scientologist. Clark had also worked with her on her preparation for the role, so there was an additional tie-in. Before going, Rena warned me to not flirt with Ms. Christensen at all, knowing that I was young and fresh off ending things with Erica back in Oklahoma. While the warning from Rena definitely scared me a bit, it only made me put more attention on it and made things a bit awkward.

We stayed at the St. Regis hotel, which is located at 16th & K streets in DC, just down the street from the White House. I shared a room with Clark and Greg. They got the beds and I had to sleep on the floor. Our budgets didn't afford for us to get our own rooms, as we were also paying for Rena's and Erika's rooms.

The first morning we met in the hotel restaurant for breakfast. I was nervous and trying not to make eye contact with Erika very much. Inevitably we had to talk and things started to lighten up a bit. That first day we had meetings with several people, including Oklahoma Senators and Representatives, and then Clark and I went back to the hotel to do work while Erika and the others went to the DEA luncheon that she had been invited to.

The next morning an interview with her ran in the Washington Post, and she also made a brief appearance on one of the local television network affiliates. She didn't directly promote Narconon in either interview, though, but instead pushed drug-free rehabilitation and education.

Downstairs in the lobby Rena had a meeting with Joy Westrum, who was also an IAS Freedom Medal winner for her work with the Second Chance prison program at Ensenada prison in Mexico. That was a rehabilitation program that fell under the ABLE program known as Criminon. She was heavily courting the National Foundation of Women Legislators and seeking funding to expand Second Chance operations in the United States. Westrum was also pictured at the DEA luncheon the previous day, which I had not known at the time.

Later that day we had a meeting scheduled with the Deputy Director of the Center for Substance Abuse Prevention (CSAP) at her office in Rockville, Maryland. After introductions, we went over to a nearby restaurant to discuss getting Narconon drug education on the CSAP approved provider list, however I was only able to stay for a short while due to a rescheduled meeting with a Congressman. I was a bit irritated because I felt it was more crucial for me to be at that meeting than to see the Congressman. On top of that, I had to walk in the chilly March mist several blocks to get to the nearest Metro station to ride the subway back into DC.

Finally, when all the meetings were done for the day, we regrouped at the hotel, changed out of our dress clothes and went to eat at a nice restaurant. After two days of work and meetings it was nice to finally relax, and all of us had gotten fairly comfortable around each other.

After dinner we walked back to the hotel, but in the lobby Erika and her mother said they wanted to take a walk around the nearby park. Clark quickly obliged and said I should join them, since Rena and Greg had other work to tend to that night. It was chilly so we grabbed a coffee to go from the lobby and headed out again. Erika and I hung back a bit, and I remember her being playful, like a kid, and that the serious meetings really weren't her style. The whole time I kept thinking that I would be in trouble with Rena for flirting, and would catch myself alternating between quiet and engaging.

Back at the hotel, the two of us stood outside our rooms for a moment to say goodnight. They had a very early flight the next morning and we were all going our separate ways. There was an extra pause for a moment, followed by an awkward half-hug. It wound up taking me a while to go to sleep as I lay on the floor of the hotel room that night, with half-cocked fantasies of dating an actress and moving to Hollywood, but duty came first - and a fear of Rena Weinberg.

Trying to Settle Down

For a few months I was just mainly focused on working again and hanging out with a handful of other staff members who were my friends. While Erica and I did occasionally have to talk for work, there was not much interaction for a while.

Later that summer, she wound up being awarded some auditing up at the church of Scientology in Kansas City for her production. Narconon was going to pay for half of it and her mother helped pay for the other half. She also went to do a course on human evaluation, which is based on L. Ron Hubbard's book Science of Survival.

While she was gone I thought about her a lot, and I was even more interested since she was becoming a Scientologist. I was going in session at the time with one of the two auditors Arrowhead was paying to have there for staff.

One of the main things in Scientology auditing is to address any overts and withholds, as they feel that these transgressions can prevent you from receiving spiritual gain. When you find one and disclose it, if the needle on the e-meter doesn't "float" (a rhythmic, sweeping motion back and forth), then you keep looking for earlier similar things you have done that you haven't disclosed yet. Many of the overts and withholds revolved around sex, and auditors are often trained to ask questions of people on the meter about their sexual habits and history.

We wound up addressing a specific time that I was with Erica, but then the greater subject came up of whether or not it was even an overt to have a relationship with her. After some badgering back and forth, I finally told my auditor that I didn't ever see anything wrong with it, that my intentions were pure because I was trying to create a more full life and that it was only someone else telling me it was unacceptable. It absolutely was not an overt for me. He asked me if I loved Erica. I said that I did. My needle floated.

Upon her return I had hinted through one of her friends that I wanted to get back together. There was something different about her. She had become more certain of herself and confident, which seemed very attractive to me at the time.

One night after work she boldly came up to my office and said, "I heard you want to start seeing each other again. Is that true?"

"Yes," I meagerly replied.

"Okay, so does that mean you're not going to join the Sea Org?"

"No."

"Then yes, I'd like to start seeing you again as well."

It was very matter-of-factly said. We were back together at the end of July.

About a month later Clark had been back at Arrowhead for some kind of visit or another. He asked me to take a walk with him, as Rena wanted him to try and develop more of a confidant-type relationship with me.

Clark had heard that I was dating Erica again and asked if it was true. I said yes and that I decided I was not going to try and join the Sea Org - that I wanted a family. He was supportive in my decision, but said that he and Rena thought that if I loved Erica that we should go ahead and get married. I wasn't sure, but told him I'd think about it.

A few days later Erica and I were talking after work and I brought up the topic. It wasn't met with resistance by her, so I just casually asked, "Well, do you want to get married?"

"Sure," she replied.

That was it. That was the proposal. It was like we were discussing whether or not we wanted to go see a movie.

During the next couple weeks word spread around our co-workers that we were going to get married, but Erica told me she didn't feel engaged without a ring. We had gone to look at rings at a jewelry store in Tulsa the Saturday after we decided, but it made her nervous to try them on. I did at least find out the basic cut and style she liked.

That week I got a call at my desk and the receptionist told me Erika Christensen was on the phone, so I took it.

"Hi Luke! I'm here with my mom and Greg in the car, and we just heard you got engaged," she said, almost with a little giggle.

"Yes, I did," I replied.

"Well congratulations!" they said, practically in unison.

I thanked them and then Erika wished me luck and that was pretty much it. After I hung up the phone I felt for a second like I had blown a potential opportunity that I had thought about a few months earlier in DC, but then I shook it off because I was excited about getting married and my job at Arrowhead.

One day I said I was going up to Tulsa to stop by U.S. Congressman John Sullivan's district office, but I actually planned on going to get her a ring. I did drop by the office and would have met if he had been available, but just only left a card and a brochure instead and headed to the jewelry store.

I didn't make much money at all being on staff at Narconon, and even as President only topped out just over $30,000 per year. I also hadn't saved any money to put down on a ring, but I picked out a brilliantly-cut round solitaire diamond, and thankfully the store let me make payments. I drove the hour and a half back to Arrowhead with the new ring in my pocket, heart pounding as I got closer to the facility and the idea of marriage started to become more real.

I made it back just before breaking for dinner. Erica came up to my office to see what we were going to for food. I got up and walked around my desk with the ring behind my back, then revealed it to her without saying a word.

She looked at it, then up at me and smiled. She put it on and it was a perfect fit. "I love it!" she exclaimed. I was proud and actually more emotional about it than she was. She headed down to the cafeteria to show her friends, because now it was finally official.

Over the next few weeks we were able to take short trips to see each other's families. I think it was sort of weird for everyone. We didn't really even know each other well enough then, and our parents seemed cautiously supportive. The world outside Narconon Arrowhead was just different. Inside the group is an entirely different reality. All you know is your job and the people you see there every day because you live and work all on the same campus.

When it came time to decide on a date, we just wanted to get it done quickly. We called the court house to schedule a time with the Justice of the Peace, whose name was Judge Bland. It was the second week of September, and we didn't want it to be on the 11th, so we picked Thursday the 12th.

For anyone involved with any Scientology-related group knows that for some reason L. Ron Hubbard decided that the week should start and end on Thursday at 2 PM. Everyone around the world tracks their weekly statistics and reports and turns them in at that time, for he didn't want momentum to be lost going into the weekend. So we went down to the Pittsburg County courthouse to see Judge Bland on Thursday morning, then after the brief ceremony, which was witnessed by Derry and his wife Michelle at the time, then we changed clothes, ate lunch and went to work in order to close out the week. It was just like business as usual.

We did wind up having a small wedding the next month in Georgia. When we got off the plane, we stopped over at the CNN headquarters in downtown Atlanta and brought a gift for Brian Denney, the PSA director, which included success stories from people who came to the program after seeing the PSAs on CNN. Then we went up to my parents house and waited for other relatives to arrive. It was a mostly-family affair, and the Scientology-style ceremony was led by Mary Rieser, who had begun her own Narconon program activities in Georgia by then.

6 JUST ANOTHER EXTENSION OF THE CHURCH

Arrowhead was a hot item in the Scientology world, and David Miscavige always wanted updated footage for events. Since Arrowhead was being displayed in these events, it had to continue to be featured with updates in order for Miscavige to show the parishioners what their money supposedly has gone toward and in order to extract more (I say "supposedly" because only a fraction of what is raised is actually spent on the things they claim).

Crews from Golden Era Productions (Gold) would drop by Arrowhead every few months, often with short notice. They would disrupt the delivery of the program for days and have a shot list, all for a few seconds' worth of actual coverage. We would have to create the appearance of extra busy spaces sometimes, such as grabbing random staff and having them sit down at a table pretending to read a book in the course room, or having a bunch of students and staff walking through the lobby all at once. They would also want updated success story interviews from recent graduates to use for more video properties as well.

Regardless of the tension it created by having the Gold crews there, we had to comply with the orders of letting them film. We weren't allowed to say no.

The Freewinds Recruiters at Arrowhead

Not long after we were married a couple, two representatives from Scientology's cruise ship called the Freewinds showed up to give a "briefing" to interested staff. It was held in the auditorium and there were approximately 50 or so staff in attendance. I recognized one of the Freewinds staff, a French woman named Claudia, because I first met her when she stopped in the Narconon Boston office when I was there a couple of years earlier.

They proceeded to give a presentation about the Freewinds and its purpose, which is to deliver Scientology's highest level, OT VIII, as well as courses and conventions. They talked about a course they offered called the Route to Infinity, which was supposed to help people's postulates (thought, will, intention, etc.) actually happen in real life.

At the end, Claudia addressed the crowd with, "Now raise your hand if you think this sounds like something you would like to do."

Erica raised her hand. I tried to pull her arm down, but it was too late. I knew the catch, they were looking for people to sell to, but Erica didn't realize this at the time.

That night Claudia came to our cabin to talk to us about going. I wasn't qualified to go, but there was a PR convention on the ship coming up and she thought it would be good for Erica to attend that along with a few other staff and to do the Route to Infinity course. Claudia said that she had already cleared it with Gary Smith for staff to attend that convention.

Erica was initially excited, right up until the point where Claudia told us how much it would cost. $3,800 for the week. Erica about fell out of her chair and immediately got defensive. "We don't have that kind of money," she said.

She was starting to get angry with Claudia for painting such a nice picture and then pulling back because it couldn't be had without the high price. She was clearly upset, and I tried to diffuse the situation by saying we did have the money. We had set up a money market account from gifts we received when we got married. There was only about $5,000 in there, but I wrote a check for the $3,800 on the spot.

Erica wound up going to the Freewinds, along with three other staff members from Arrowhead for the PR convention just a couple weeks later.

Scientology's International Landlord's Office

Narconon Arrowhead doesn't own its building or the property. As stated earlier, it was purchased and renovated with money given by the IAS. At first ABLE owned the property and Arrowhead paid the $30,000 per month in rent to them, but not long after that the ownership was transferred to a separate property holding company owned and controlled by the church.

The original renovation was overseen by the Church's International Landlord office, but it soon became apparent that at the rate Arrowhead was growing there would be more space needed. In addition, we needed a medical detox facility to properly service people withdrawing from many different kinds of substances, and had been referring them out to other detox centers for services. Medically supervised detox costs on average $500-$1,000 per day, so this was also a financial decision.

The liability was a greater issue legally. Per an executive briefing issued by Gary Smith later:

"Currently, Narconon Arrowhead is faced with some legal exposure with the way we are handling new public that show up in the program requiring medically supervised detox services. Narconon Arrowhead is classified as a 'health care facility' in the eyes of the certifying and accreditation agencies that govern drug rehabilitation programs. Therefore, once Narconon intake people give the go ahead to a new arrival to come to the program and they arrive at our door step the organization is responsible to ensure that each student's health and well being are provided for while they are in the program. If we have accepted a new student and they need medical care that is not delivered at Narconon, then Narconon is responsible to find those services from outside agencies and make every effort to encourage the person to take advantage of those services.

"In the case of sending a person to an outside medical detox unit Narconon has the responsibility of getting a person to medical detox once we have determined that is what they need. Even though we are referring to an outside agency, Narconon can still be held responsible if some life threatening situation happens to a person in the hands of the outside agency. This is because Narconon initially accepted the person, had the person transported to Narconon Arrowhead and then Narconon selected the outside agency and referred the person to that agency."

There were also other situations that were thought had to be addressed, such as the International Training Center. Scientology promoted (and still does promote) Narconon Arrowhead as the International Training Center (ITC) of for the Narconon network, but in reality very few people completed training at Arrowhead outside of their own staff. There were delegates that would come, or there would be a few pockets of staff here and there, but for the most part the ITC was actually a non-existent joke. Arrowhead was also made out by the church to be like the headquarters of Narconon, but Narconon International in Los Angeles is.

An additional building they wanted was a Personal Integrity Center, which was also referred to as the ethics camp. There were a lot of people getting suspended from Arrowhead, quite in addition to those who just left without completing. In a PowerPoint presentation created by Arrowhead executives in 2003, it stated that 55 people were suspended from the program in the first six months of that year and had over $95,000 in refund requests during the same time period. Those refund requests didn't include the ones from people who came and just decided to leave on their own.

The theory was to "suspend" problem students over to the ethics camp to try to retain them longer in a more controlled environment so that they could also get and keep more of the income from those students if they had not fully paid or had requested refunds. This theory was devised after the implementation of a separate ethics course room that was credited with reducing the number of suspensions. They averaged more than 10 per month in 2002. The registrars (sales department) were literally driving in more people than the program could waste, as more than 100 suspensions per year then was more people than some centers had as their entire client count for a whole year.

In the midst of all of this, new expansion plans had been drawn up to build additional facilities on the property, and at first Miscavige told Gary Smith he would approve another IAS grant for the new construction, and sent out representatives from the Landlord's Office yet again. These two Sea Org members actually spent months living at the facility and had their own office and everything, working out design and space planning. There were some modifications done to the main building and some more upgrades done to several cabins, though that was it.

Eventually the IAS repeatedly denied the grant to build new buildings. Arrowhead on its own then qualified for a construction loan based on revenue, but the trick was trying to convince the church to allow it, especially with Narconon International in opposition of putting a medical detox facility on site.

Per the same executive briefing on the expansion plans written by Gary Smith, if the center continued to grow at the pace it was and filled all the new spaces to capacity, it would have generated $560,000 per week. Operating costs were estimated at capacity to only be $210,000 with the expansion, leaving a projected net income of $350,000 per week at capacity.

Arrowhead was averaging $200,000 per week in 2003, with $120,000 in weekly expenses, still leaving more than $80,000 net.

The briefing showed that Narconon Arrowhead would increase from 40% profitability to 63% profitability. Quite an interesting angle when it is supposed to be a non-profit, but when you're dealing with Scientology, you have to speak in money terms like any other corporation.

Making Headway and Being Exploited

My job description was to make Narconon broadly publicized, well-known and accepted. We had been growing steadily in the realm of people looking for something other than their local rehab online, but we definitely had not gotten much further than a truce within much of the treatment field. I wanted to find a way to change that, and came to the conclusion that the only way to do that was to start making friends in the field.

Early on I had attended the Community Anti-Drug Coalitions of America (CADCA) conference in DC along with Yvonne Rodgers from Narconon East US and Sue Birkenshaw from Narconon International. I also attended the Southeastern Conference on Addictive Disorders (SECAD) in Atlanta, but needed to find something locally to be involved in to gain more acceptance and understanding within the state of Oklahoma.

I found an organization called the Oklahoma Substance Abuse Services Alliance (OSASA), which was basically a statewide providers group that consisted of most of the major treatment and prevention programs working on advocacy and public policy together. I joined OSASA one day at a monthly meeting and was pleasantly surprised at the welcome I received.

Most of the providers had heard of Narconon, but didn't know much about it at all, and were pleased that there was an attempt to actually open up and interact with other facility executives. I think the biggest reason that it went so smoothly is because I was there to learn and make friends. I didn't come in with the attitude of being above them all in some way, even though that was the consensus back at the Arrowhead campus.

At first Gary and Vicki Smith thought I was wasting my time with OSASA, not understanding really the valuable connections that were being made and how important it was for acceptance at a state level. At the time the President of OSASA was Paul Hackler, who was the Executive Director of The Oaks Rehabilitation Center in McAlester, our neighbor whom hadn't even been approached previously.

The immediate past President was Kyle McGraw from A Chance to Change Foundation in Oklahoma City (who later was appointed to the Director of Substance Abuse Services for the Department of Human Services in Oklahoma) and the President-elect was June Ross from 12 & 12 in Tulsa. There were many other members and it was like the who's who of treatment and prevention in the state.

Since Narconon had such a prominent web presence, I volunteered to be part of a marketing committee and worked with one of our staff members to develop a website for OSASA. They were very appreciative. Acceptance was going well, but even greater was that there was a lot of interaction with state officials, from legislators to Dept. of Mental Health and Substance Abuse Services staff. All of a sudden Gary, Clark, Rena and others began to take notice, because it was a level of acceptance within the state that hadn't been previously reached, and it was also an informational feeder line regarding state policies and regulations, which was very important considering the history of Narconon in the state.

My involvement in OSASA continued, and since I was so eager, the membership actually nominated me and voted me onto the executive committee to serve for three years and was in line to be the President of OSASA in 2005 had I continued to stay involved.

As a member of the executive committee, there was an additional monthly meeting to attend, and we usually rotated holding them at each other's facilities rather than the same place of the regular membership meetings. Interest was expressed by the committee to come out and see Arrowhead, and so one month I got the other executive members out to tour and had a chance to give them the PR explanation of the facility. They were impressed with the size of the operation and of course the finances, because they knew our annual budget. Not many places in the state came close to Arrowhead's revenue, and certainly not in terms of residential beds. We were generating more than $8 million per year by then, and still growing.

All in all, I was very impressed with the members of OSASA, including their sincere desire to help people and affect positive change socially and politically. I truly enjoyed my time and opportunity working with the leaders of the member facilities from around the state.

More Congressional Activity

Scientology had hired its own full-time lobbyist, Greg Mitchell. I had attended a meeting in the conference room above Rena's office at ABLE Int in LA regarding Scientology's social betterment representation at the Capitol in D.C. Present at the meeting were Gary Smith, Deputy Commanding Officer of the Office of Special Affairs (OSA) Kurt Weiland and his assistant, Greg Mitchell, ABLE Director of Development Rubina Qureshi, Clark Carr, Rena Weinberg and me.

Rena had told me prior to the meeting to basically stay silent and observe since Kurt Weiland was going to be there, which I did for the most part. However, they had gotten some things mixed up and I interjected regarding the scene in Oklahoma. I explained my position within OSASA and the state of affairs, as well as my understanding of the political landscape in the addiction treatment field at the time.

The main political goals included gaining more acceptance and support, but also to find budgetary earmarks to be able to get public funding for Scientology activities through ABLE programs. Mitchell was supposed to keep an eye out for possible funding sources.

To say that OSA had involvement in the PR and legal aspects of Narconon would be an understatement.

Cruise's Special Guest

In the spring of 2003 we got a call from Celebrity Centre International (CC Int). Tom Cruise had a personal friend that he wanted to do the full Narconon program at Arrowhead. It was a big deal and everyone was expected to drop what we were doing to cater to this need. That day a private jet flew in to McAlester carrying Cruise's friend, then-Vice President of CC Int Maria Ferrara and one of Tom's top personal staff Andrea Doven.

Maria and Andrea immediately assumed power when they walked into my office and started ordering things around. They spotted an end suite with a great view of the lake and wanted the three students that were staying in it to be removed and relocated for this one guy. They wanted to room heavily cleaned and all of the best furniture put in there, including brand-new linens.

This started to cause quite an uproar among other staff and especially students. One of the things they all had to sign when starting the program was that they didn't believe someone should receive special treatment because of his or her financial or social position, yet here it was blatantly happening to cater to someone.

Jeannie Trahant is an IAS Freedom Medal Winner as well as reportedly the first female Narconon graduate and an OT VIII. She was used to be the personal facilitator of this guy's program and worked with him and his twin throughout the entire thing. Incidentally, Jeannie was also the person who Juliette Lewis credits with helping her get through the steps of the Narconon program many years ago.

Cruise's friend was polite, humble and not recognizable since he was a business man rather than an artist. Even most of the staff never knew who he really was. He was not the one demanding any of the special attention, and it actually created a situation where other students started to resent him. The actions of Maria and Andrea made it an unhealthy environment for him to be able to do the program.

The situation had gotten so undesirable inside the building with the mess they created to cater to this guy, that they wound up moving him down to have his own special cabin to live in, like staff members had. While some got even more upset about this at first, it at least solved the problem in the building since the other students got their room back and it eventually quieted down. However, not only was it against the licensing laws of the facility to house a client somewhere else on the property, but this was also the first time I recalled major HIPAA (patient privacy laws) violations as well, because daily reports on this guy were sent to Celebrity Centre and Tom Cruise's staff so they knew what was going on with him and how he was progressing. It was a complete violation of his confidentiality perpetrated by two IAS Freedom Medal winners - Jeannie Trahant and Gary Smith.

I hadn't been around as long so I didn't have nearly as much interaction and therefore wasn't required to do the reporting. However, I was occasionally asked to do favors for him by Jeannie or Gary. One day I took this guy and his twin into town to get ice cream, while another day I took them to play golf.

One day Cruise flew in to meet with his friend. He came by himself and didn't enter the facility. Gary picked him up in McAlester and they had a private meeting in the cabin where his friend was staying. Gary told me that on the way back to the airport Cruise asked him to pull into the Burger King. Tom tried to order something that wasn't on the menu and they wouldn't make it for him specially, so he got something else instead. When they got to the window, he leaned over and looked in to the drive through window and said, "Are you sure you can't do that for me?" Gary said the girl working was stunned and couldn't believe her eyes. Her only response was, "I'm sorry." Gary paid and they left, and to this day I bet none of her employees believed her that Tom Cruise was at the Burger Kind drive through in McAlester, OK.

After Cruise's friend eventually completed the program, I only ever saw him one other time at Celebrity Centre in Los Angeles, though would sometimes get updates from Gary about his status. If he ever really became a Scientologist, it was apparently short-lived.

More Celebrity Centre Involvement

The fact was that Narconon Arrowhead violated the confidentiality of multiple clients by reporting on their progress to the church of Scientology, and specifically CC Int. In addition to two people that Cruise was personally responsible for bringing to Arrowhead, there were other celebrities who had also referred friends or family members.

There was a woman associated with Priscilla Presley, a young man tied to Chick Corea, a guy connected to Louis Farrakhan, an older woman who was connected to someone from the Rat Pack, and others.

This was a point of contention for me, as they demanded daily progress reports on most of these people, if not at least weekly.

Most of them I didn't have to deal with, but it was incredibly invasive, disruptive for work and dealing with CC Int staff was just a pain in the ass.

Efforts to Be Legitimized via Fringe Endorsements

An African American Episcopal (AME) minister named Rev. James McLaughlin and his wife Cleo had gotten a newsletter about Narconon somehow. James was involved in outreach programs through his local ministry and Cleo thought that Narconon might be something they could use in the Houston, TX area.

They wound up coming to Arrowhead and taking some introductory courses. Vicki Smith had cultivated the relationship and saw the opportunity to exploit a black Christian relationship as a PR move. Along with representatives from a church in Oklahoma, the McLaughlins paid a very small fee to do the beginning TRs course as well as the Learning Improvement course. It was supposed to take a week and the courses were done in the staff and trainee course room.

In the middle of that week, the delegation from the Oklahoma ministry left because they felt they were being indoctrinated into Scientology and had overheard staff reading Scientology references aloud as well as spotted many Scientology books in the course room. Despite my efforts to convince them otherwise, they left (good for them).

The McLaughlins, however, were much more drawn into it. They wound up applying for a Narconon license and were even present for the next Narconon International Executive Director's conference that was held Easter weekend.

They soon did get their license and opened up a small Narconon First Step center in the Houston area, where Gary Smith and Clark Carr were present for the opening ceremony. This venture didn't last long though, and Cleo wound up joining staff at Arrowhead while James was used as a pawn in things such as various conferences for Narconon and Scientology since he was an AME minister open to using Hubbard practices. Both of them have been frequently propped up in front of camera lenses to try and "prove" Narconon's diversity.

Visits from Dignitaries

One of the functions of my position and office was to host dignitaries and include tours and detailed briefings for them, especially with the intention of trying to get Narconon and other Hubbard-related programs implemented into more areas and organizations.

As Gary Smith stated, "This in turn will produce Opinion Leader status for Narconon Arrowhead and the Narconon network. The influence and power generated by these dissemination activities will then be channeled towards influencing the 'rule makers' that regulated the world-wide drug rehabilitation industry to:

"1. Reset the drug treatment standards and regulations that govern the operation and dissemination of rehabilitation and prevention services so they align with LRH's tech.

"2. Create even more demand for result-driven solutions for the world's drug epidemic thus expanding the exportation of LRH drug rehabilitation technology even further into the fabric of society."

The intention was never to really cooperate, but instead to manipulated and control.

Some of the dignitaries who came from out of state and even out of the country included a representative from the Filipino DEA, Utah Attorney General Mark Shurtleff, Jordanian police delegates, Mayor Connie de la Garza of Harlingen, TX and others.

Most of them, if not all, were either interested in helping people in their areas more by getting some type of Narconon program set up in their city, state or country.

Legislative and Certification Work

Somewhere around this time the laws had changed in the state of Oklahoma for the licensing of treatment centers. Previously, Narconon was allowed to operate by getting a Health Department facility inspection and occupancy permit combined with accreditation from the Commission for Accreditation of Rehabilitation Facilities (CARF). A legal opinion was provided to Arrowhead that the Health Department would no longer be involved in the licensing process at all, and that Oklahoma law dictated that unless you are a faith-based program, you must fall under the oversight of a state agency. This meant that Narconon had to seek out certification from the Oklahoma Department of Mental Health and Substance Abuse Services (ODMHSAS) or work on changing the governing laws in the state.

Narconon's history in Oklahoma was not a pleasant one. Back in the late 80's Narconon set out to open a treatment center in the state by signing a 25-yr lease of the Chilocco Indian School. Scientology created ABLE back then and invested a lot of time, money and resources into opening "the largest residential rehabilitation center in the world." They arrogantly came in and started flaunting their resources and using celebrities to cause much fanfare (see a pattern?). When they got their inspection from the Department of Mental Health, the Board denied certification.

Narconon had to transfer all their students immediately, and could only provide services to Native Americans since they were on their land. A huge media and legal battle ensued, complete with Scientology using its usual dirty tactics to threaten and coerce local Newkirk, OK reporter Bob Lobsinger as well as Mayor Garry Bilger. Oklahoma became a Scientology battleground.

Eventually they discovered that the law allowed them to receive outside accreditation in lieu of certification from the Department of Mental Health, which is how they found CARF. Many conspiracy theorists believe that the church somehow influenced the CARF surveyors for accreditation, as one of them was a guy named Kent McGregor, who went on to become very active in working with Narconon.

Once Narconon received CARF accreditation, they dropped

the lawsuits and called a truce with the state in 1992. Fast forward more than a decade later and they were faced with another possible situation, and nobody wanted to enter into a costly legal battle again, including the state.

Many resources were called to investigate possible solutions to the problem we were facing back then. While that research was going on, we began looking to gain favor with many state legislators in case they were needed as leverage within the state. Also, since I had developed many connections with other treatment centers being on the executive committee with OSASA, resources were being mined to begin friendly dialogue with the Department of Mental Health and Substance Abuse Services.

One of the initial actions was to compare all of the current CARF requirements with the state regulations to see how close to compliance the facility could be. At the same time OSA was guiding Gary Smith, Director of Legal Affairs Mike St. Amand and Lead Counsel Sandy McNabb on hiring an attorney with political clout. That search ultimately ended in the hiring of David Riggs, who formerly served in the state legislature. Gary also called an old friend of his named Joan Hastings for advice, who was also a former legislator.

Around this same time there was a push to create the Oklahoma Drug and Alcohol Licensing Board, which would eventually make it a requirement for Licensed Drug and Alcohol Counselors to have Masters Degrees in a psychology-related field. Up until that point there was the Oklahoma Drug and Alcohol Professional Counselor's Association, which issued counseling certifications as a branch of the International Certification & Reciprocity Consortium (IC&RC). Since it was already a problem for Narconon counselors, most of whom had no degrees or certifications, raising the bar and requirements in the definition of professional treatment staff presented the possibility of an even bigger issue to deal with.

In early May of 2003 Gary Smith and Mike St. Amand convinced Representative Terry Harrison and Senator Frank Shurden to present a concurrent resolution that supported Narconon Arrowhead. Usually things like that simply slip through and get unanimous approvals in on both floors without a real vote, but it narrowly passed the Senate after some questioning about licensing issues, and then met opposition on the floor of the House and was defeated, primarily due to Narconon's connection with Scientology. The slick little back door pat on the back that Gary and Mike tried to engineer backfired and made Narconon look worse in the eyes of the legislature and wound up getting press coverage in the Tulsa World.

I was then called in to help run damage control. We constructed a legislative briefing pack that was complete with letters of support from schools, churches, other non-profit organizations, and any other type of elected official we had. We also included drawings of the expansion plans that were in place at the time and results from an economic impact study with the projections of how much money Arrowhead was bringing into the local economy directly and indirectly.

I scheduled two days out at the Capitol on Oklahoma City. I had specific people to try and meet with and personally give the briefing packs to, while the rest were just dropped off. On May 7th and 8th I wound up visiting with the following legislators and/or their assistants: Terry Harrison, Ray Miller, Frank Shurden, Richard Lerblance, Kevin Calvey, Tad Jones, Lance Cargill, Bill Paulk, John Wright, Wayne Pettigrew, Todd Hiett, Thad Balkman, Joan Greenwood, Larry Adair, Mike O'Neal, Carolyn Coleman, Danny Hilliard and Fred Perry.

Despite the opposition, everyone I met with was cordial and didn't really bring up any direct problems with me. While there weren't any open hostilities displayed, we weren't exactly met with open arms either.

On May 12th I went back and this time with Gary and Vicki Smith as well as our Director of Community Relations, Peggy Bunda. We continued distributing the briefing packs and met with several more legislators and/or their assistants, including Mike Tyler, Lucky Lamons, Barbara Staggs, Chris Hastings, Ray McCarter, Frank Davis, Jerry Ellis, Kris Steele and John Trebilcock.

After the news story, a long-time critic of Narconon, Barbara Graham, began contacting more Oklahoma legislators and sending information to them about Narconon and Scientology, so I went back to the Capitol on the 14th and brought Peggy with me again to have a few follow-up meetings since we found out about Barbara Graham. OSA had also prepared a special "Dead Agent" (DA) letter about Ms. Graham trying to smear her so the legislators wouldn't listen to her. Dead Agenting is a term meaning to discredit a foe. This DA material was only given to a few people, and it was information for them to use when other legislators mentioned the letters received from Ms. Graham. It was a personal attack on her, something that OSA specializes in and a tactic that Hubbard used for the Guardian's Office (GO) before that.

Later that year, ODMHSAS Deputy Commissioner for Substance Abuse Ben Brown approached me after an OSASA meeting. He wasn't happy.

"Listen," he said, "tell your people we are willing to provide whatever technical assistance you need to help get your shop certified. There is no need to go around the issue. Nobody is looking for a fight here."

Unbeknownst to me, Mike and Gary were busy with Riggs and others trying to talk directly to Brown's boss, Commissioner Terry Cline. Apparently I wasn't given full OSA clearance by the church, so they still held secret meetings regarding legal matters occasionally. I reported to him what Ben Brown said and also displayed my disapproval for even putting me in a position where I didn't know what was going on, but hell, these guys had been working together for decades, and I was just some kid.

Other Narconon Centers

At the end of May 2003 Narconon Warner Springs/San Diego/Sunshine Summit had its grand opening ceremony. I rode in the car with Rena and her assistant Lisa to help out with the event. I was mainly on standby to help answer questions as well as help write a draft of the press release. Clark Carr was there as well as other Narconon International employees.

In addition to the local dignitaries or representatives,

Scientologist Nancy Cartwright came to lend her support too, where she specifically highlighted Narconon drug prevention activities and handed out Narconon's 10 Things Your Friends May Not Know About Drugs booklet, which of course is based on erroneous or at least exaggerated information from Hubbard.

Narconon first incorporated in Southern California, Los Angeles specifically, in 1970 by William Benitez, Henning Heldt and Arte Maren. Heldt and Maren were members of the Church of Scientology Guardian's Office (GO). The GO soon wrested control of the organization for the church, forcing Benitez to sign away his rights to the name and trademarks, yet to this day still pretends it is not controlled by the church.

As a side note, for those who aren't familiar with the GO, it ran many illegal operations and Heldt, Hubbard's wife Mary Sue and other members wound up serving time in prison for their infiltration of the U.S. Government. The GO was later disbanded and replaced with the Office of Special Affairs (OSA), which continues the dirty work for the church. Many members of the old GO were kicked out of the Sea Org and not allowed to return, though many remained Scientologists and stayed active in other ways. One of these people was Phil Hart, who has been the Executive Director of Narconon International for many years and is an OT VIII in the church.

ABLE was also the reincarnation of the GO's Social Coordination Bureau, and several GO members moved over to become ABLE staff members, remaining in the Sea Org.

Narconon's entire history is quite varied, though this is not an archival attempt at all. I merely wanted to give a bit of background.

Narconon in Los Angeles eventually moved to Newport Beach. It's Executive Director for many years, Jeannie Trahant. Narconon Newport Beach eventually closed down due to overcrowding and angry neighbors who wanted them out. The facility folded into the Warner Springs center as well as a newer Facility in Nevada. They have since opened a small residence in Huntington Beach also. To escape the "black PR" online, Narconon Southern California, now led by Jeannie's ex-husband Larry Trahant, likes to change the names of the facilities, and even recently changed the names of it's sub-group into the Narconon Fresh Start Centers.

Narconon Stone Hawk

In one of my other roles as sort of Ambassador to other Narconon's, I flew up to Kalamazoo, Michigan at the end of June 2003 with one of my friends and fellow staff members, Jean Lafitte. Jean had been my roommate for a few weeks before we moved to Arrowhead, and he and I frequently worked on different projects. He had a background in television production and editing before coming to LA. He was smart and talented and we often debated different topics and theories for fun.

We drove to Battle Creek, were Per Wickstrom (pronounced like pair), a graduate from Chilocco, and his wife Kate were having the grand opening ceremony for their new facility called Narconon Stone Hawk.

They had already upset a bunch of people at Arrowhead by trying to steal staff members from them and offering them more money to work up in Michigan, but we were there as a goodwill gesture. Besides, the church kept portraying Arrowhead as an "emanation point for new Narconon centers" and so it was important for us to make an appearance. Rena and Clark were also there, and Jean and I were there just as back-up and to lend a hand if needed.

We first met over at the Battle Creek Org, where Scientology staff and parishioners were gathered to also help volunteer for the ceremony. Then when the event started a couple local news crews showed up. Clark asked me to be ready in case I needed to fill in so that the reporters wouldn't just ask random people questions. Kate Wickstrom saw this and was furious, she didn't want anyone stealing her coverage, rather than being thankful for the back-up support.

Once the event was done, we went back to Oklahoma, but the problems with Stone Hawk, and specifically Per and Kate, only continued. They wound up getting embroiled in several lawsuits from unhappy family members, were featured on numerous radio shows hosted by Vince Daniels and they found themselves in major financial trouble. They were growing only out of fraud, not out of good service or helping people. Kate wanted out.

During one trip to Los Angeles, I overheard Bobby Wiggins talking with Phil Hart about Per and Kate. Bobby said, "If Kate doesn't get on the Bridge then it won't work having her there."

"Why would she reach for Scientology when her husband keeps relapsing?" Phil replied, "She doesn't have a good example of it working."

Problems continued to escalate, but they kept bringing people in and getting paid so they acquired a second facility a couple years later. However, they continued to have mounting problems. Per and Kate got divorced and she threatened to sue him and Narconon International. To make her go away, Narconon international borrowed money from people, including Arrowhead and other Narconon centers, to pay her the amount they agreed on.

As with many people who settle with any of Scientology's branches, Kate had to sign a non-disclosure agreement in order to get her money. This happens very frequently with Narconon centers. However, if people are subpoenaed for a court case, they still have to testify under oath and give the details of any matter they were involved in.

Per Wickstrom was eventually stripped of his Narconon license because of the continued problems. Stone Hawk was shut down and reopened as Narconon Freedom Center, operating only out of the second building.

The troubled story of Narconon in Michigan continues to this day. Per Wickstrom operates two other treatment centers and a detox clinic now in his other buildings. One is called A Forever Recovery, and the other is called Best Drug Rehabilitation. The first program is supposed to offer multiple methods of treatment for people to be able to choose their own path, but per multiple eyewitness accounts, the second facility operates by giving actual Scientology courses to its clients - something it clearly doesn't admit to in any of its promotional materials.

When A Forever Recovery first opened I would write reports

to Narconon International and ABLE about Per Wickstrom stealing clients away from Narconon. Phil Hart continued to cover for him though because Per was paying back the money Narconon Int paid his ex-wife. Phil told me personally that he wanted Per back in the Narconon network because, despite all of his ethical shortcomings, he knew how to make money.

At least two people who worked for Per Wickstrom have died in recent years. David Vantrease committed suicide in 2010 and the Stephen Ballard died of a drug overdose. Per Wickstrom has proudly given over a million dollars to the IAS, per its own publication, and the church continues to allow him to defraud people as long as he keeps forking over large sums of cash to Scientology.

As a side note, Kate wasn't the only Executive Director who was paid off to avoid a lawsuit. A couple years prior to that Frank Montero was running Narconon in northern California. He was a former staff member at Chilocco and then went out to CA. The center had grown under his watch and was making more money. He got the Board there to agree to a contract extension guaranteeing him a reported salary of $150,000 per year for another three years. One day I was talking on the phone with Clark Carr and he explained that Narconon Int had gone in and fired Frank and that they had to pay out his contract to avoid a wrongful termination and discrimination lawsuit. In Narconon land, his crimes were that he was dating "A Psych" and refused to go to a Scientology church for handling and correction. Incidentally, the current Executive Director of Narconon Vista Bay there in northern California receives more than $250,000 per year, as does her husband, according to IRS Form 990 reports.

David Miscavige Visits Arrowhead

In late July 2003, I flew up to St. Louis, MO along with Gary Smith and Mike Gosselin to attend the grand opening of the Applied Scholastics International Spanish Lake facility. Applied Scholastics is a branch of ABLE that licenses L. Ron Hubbard's

Study Tech that is used for learning and tutoring.

The ceremony was bigger than Arrowhead's grand opening and included Scientology celebrities such as Tom Cruise, Jenna Elfman, Anne Archer and Isaac Hayes. There was additional excitement because Scientology leader David Miscavige was also going to be in attendance.

The general audience was buzzing about the fact that Tom Cruise actually got up and spoke. He delivered a speech about overcoming dyslexia and getting his pilot's license. However, he was followed by L. Ron Hubbard's biographer (and David Miscavige's speech writer) Dan Sherman. Sherman spoke for way too long in his effeminate bubble-throat voice about some such aspect of Hubbard's life and lost most of the crowed in his long-windedness.

After the speeches and tours, a reception was held in a large tent complete with catering and the Golden Era musicians (Scientology band). During the reception Gary Smith went up to David Miscavige, thanked him, and invited him to come down to Narconon Arrowhead since they were in the middle part of the country already. A few minutes later Miscavige's assistant told Gary that they would be coming down for a visit after all.

The next day we flew back to Oklahoma and prepped the staff for the arrival of Miscavige and his entourage. The entire place went through a deep cleaning and "white glove" inspection. A few students were also selected to share their stories with Miscavige, including two attractive young women and a young man that was there on a scholarship to gain favor with Louis Farrakhan from the Nation of Islam.

Miscavige and his crew wound up coming the day after that. They flew into the tiny airport in McAlester on a private jet. Present with him were ABLE Executive Director Laurie Zurn, Rena Weinberg, Dan Sherman, Tommy Davis, Inspector General Marty Rathbun, Shelly Miscavige, and an additional person or two.

Gary and Mike drove a white passenger van down to the airport, and I followed in my car. All of the guests were able to pile into the van except one - Dan Sherman, gray mullet and all. On the way to the facility Sherman proceeded to tell me that Narconon didn't really handle someone's "drug case", it just put it at bay for a while. He said that the only way to truly handle it is to do the Scientology Drug Rundown, the New Era Dianetics (NED) Drug Rundown, and eventually the OT Drug Rundown. What a great thing to say to the President of the flagship Narconon facility - that it doesn't do what it thinks it does! Little did I or he know at the time, but it turns out that he was more right than either of us realized, at least about the first part.

Before arriving at the center we stopped at the overlook in the state park and everybody hopped out to check out the surroundings, with half of us lighting up a smoke - Miscavige included. He stood there looking proud of "his" accomplishment while Gary pointed out the various parts of the property.

Once we got into the facility, select staff members were chosen to explain their jobs to Miscavige and the rest of the group as we went through a tour of the whole building. Then we came to the Program Support Services (PSS) area, where the three or four students sat waiting to share their stories. Miscavige sat down in a circle of chairs with them while everyone else stood around the outside. I was in the doorway. First each of them took their turns talking to him, and then they asked him what his story was, and he talked about having asthma as a kid and that was how he got introduced to Dianetics - as a form of therapy for it.

After we left PSS then we started walking across the building to go upstairs to my office. On the way, two of his assistance had dropped back a bit and were whispering to themselves. Miscavige noticed this and stopped. He turned around and said loudly, as if scolding them, "Is there a problem?" They quickly stopped whispering and hurried to catch up. I remembered this as being odd, for why would he speak downwardly to them in a loud voice at all for simply talking to each other, let alone act that way in front of others and at a casual visit. Most of the members of the entourage were in jeans or some other type of relaxed outfit. I think his assistants were the only ones wearing their Sea Org uniforms.

While in my office having coffee and snacks, Vicki Smith began showing Miscavige and the others different things we had done in recent years that she had documented in large binders that were like her form of scrap booking. These binders included pictures of the move and grand opening, visitors and dignitaries, community events, press coverage and other things.

In the middle of this, Tommy Davis asked Gary if there was a place where they could smoke privately since Miscavige didn't like to be seen smoking publicly, and he said they could go to his office. So Gary and Miscavige and a couple others went in to his little office to smoke, while I stood outside the door on the walkway talking with Rena and Laurie.

By the time everything was wrapping up, it started to get dark. On the way out the door we paused in front of the building for pictures with the Narconon Arrowhead logo in the background. Then Gary drove them all back to the airport himself. At the time I thought it was such a cool day and that I was lucky to have participated in that occasion. Gary told me when he got back that it was a rare treat to have so much time with Miscavige, especially in an informal setting like that. Gary was in complete awe of him.

A couple weeks later, Gary received a package with a note from Miscavige and several pictures of the various groups together from that day. The one I was given had Gary and Vicki Smith, Rena Weinberg, Laurie Zurn, David Miscavige and me. I still have the picture and recently found it. I scanned it and posted it online, where it has been shared and reposted on various forums and blogs that are critical of Narconon and Scientology.

The Celebrity Centre Gala

The Church of Scientology Celebrity Centre International holds its annual gala in August. It is a way for it to show off its accomplishments to friends and guests and is also used as a Hollywood recruiting tool. In August of 2003 there was an extra display set up at CC Int that was sort of like an L. Ron Hubbard mini life exhibition, which had large panels detailing the various parts.

I was asked to be stationed at the Narconon panel to explain to the guests who would be touring through so they would know what the program was about. Additional panels included ones for more ABLE groups and other aspects of Dianetics and Scientology such as an e-meter demonstration. I had to be there hours before the actual event started, which was mostly a black tie affair.

I had been hanging out and talking with Bob Adams, who is a former NFL football player and had recently joined the Sea Org as the Vice President of ABLE. We had been talking about steroids and were given a binder with pictures of dignitaries and prominent Hollywood people that were expected to attend. Below each picture was a short description of who they were and what they did, so that we knew to watch out for them and ensure that they really got extra attention coming through the displays.

Just then a handful of people walked by, including Giovanni Ribisi and Tom Cruise, who had long hair and a beard, probably left over in case there were any re-shoots needed on The Last Samurai. They each nodded and said hi as they passed, but no further conversation.

As it got closer to the start of the event and people began arriving, we were told that we needed to leave the speaking part of the event a few minutes early and be ready at the displays before everyone else got there.

Susan Watson was the President of CC Int then, and she was the host for the event. As I stood there I saw Dr. Alfonso Paredes and his wife. I had met them before when they came out to Arrowhead. He was the retired psychiatrist and professor from UCLA who was on Narconon's Advisory Board. He wasn't a Scientologist, but his son was, and I was told that the only way his son was allowed to do Scientology services was if he handled his dad to not practice psychiatry anymore, not advocate for psychiatric drugs, and to do something in support of Scientology activities, which is how the Narconon bit came about. Paredes later wrote a short program evaluation in September of that year that is still used to this day to show parents, family members and others that Narconon was psychiatrically reviewed, but of course they leave out the part of his connection to Scientology. The fact is that very few people endorse Narconon or anything related to Scientology without a connection of some sort.

Next I was introduced to a gentleman wearing very expensive-looking glasses and a designer tuxedo. We started talking and he found out where I worked. He asked what all Narconon really does in the program, and he was surprised that every graduate wasn't referred to the nearest Scientology church upon program completion. He had very little understanding about Narconon except for the church events that promote it to its membership. I found this to be true for most Scientologists, as the events are a key part of the propaganda machine.

Once the guest speakers began, I took off to go over to the display to get ready. About fifteen minutes later people started to stroll through, and in the background the Golden Era Musicians band was playing and there was a very nice buffet and tables set up for the attendees.

I spent the next couple of hours talking to people about Narconon, some of whom were Scientologists who didn't really know much about it, and other people were guests so it was all completely new to them.

During this time a church member came up to me and started telling me how she sent her brother to Narconon a couple times years ago, and that he stayed clean for a little bit, but he needed to come back to Narconon and they didn't have any more money to pay for the program again. She asked if there was anything I could do, but I told her to call Gary Smith since he was over the daily operations.

Shortly after that Erika Christensen appeared, this time with both of her parents. I suddenly started feeling really weird and embarrassed as images of DC and then the phone call ran through my mind quickly and I looked down at my wedding ring. She proceeded to tell me that her brothers were making short skateboarding films and I congratulated her on her rising career. Then her mother grabbed a digital camera and said she wanted a picture of us. We posed next to each other, with me fighting back a nervous sweat as I put my arm around her for the picture. Then I shook all their hands again and they continued on through the display. My wife was already very jealous and the last thing I needed was that picture to surface. Thankfully it never did.

By the time the entire event was over I was exhausted and starving. My feet were killing me as I started walking to my hotel, which was just a few blocks away. When I got back I didn't have the energy to sit in the 101 Coffee Shop, so I got some peanut M&M's and a Coke out of the vending machine instead. I was spent.

Narconon Arrowhead's 2nd Anniversary Event

While I had put together a meager anniversary event for Arrowhead in 2002, it wasn't nearly the size or scope of what was needed, per Clark and Rena. There wasn't enough fanfare, according to them, for the centerpiece of the Narconon network.

We began planning much earlier for the 2003 event, and a lot more money was set aside for the expenses. I came up with the concepts, location and speakers, and Vicki Smith added some of her personal touches - some of which were beneficial and some where just for her own satisfaction and got in the way.

Vicki Smith wanted to do a special recognition of early Narconon graduates and do her own internal event, which ate up a chunk of my event budget and made my office look worse to the financial planning committee. She wound up flying in several people from around the country and overseas. She also wanted the Jive Aces to come and perform, which is a Scientology swing band from England (recently featured on the UK's X Factor). I will admit that they put on a good show, but she wound up flying all of them in at great expense. Vicki really wanted her own little party with some of her favorite people and old friends, as well as to acknowledge her husband. She printed plaques for the graduates from the 1970's who were in attendance and they were given out after the regular program graduates got their certificates that Friday night.

For the actual anniversary event, we wound up renting the entire McAlester Expo Center. Since I was so heavily involved in OSASA, I was able to invite other treatment center providers and recovery organizations from around the state. I also opened it up for them to be able to set up their own display booths or exhibits in addition to some other community organizations to talk more about their services. The theme was working together to address the problems we faced as a whole.

After seeing other Scientology celebrities present at the Applied Scholastics event, Priscilla Presley said she wanted to participate in something and agreed to speak at our anniversary event. This meant a better opportunity for press coverage, but also was a distraction because of the extra handling that needed to go on to facilitate her presence.

We rented a lake house for her, of course had to pay for last-minute first-class airfare, had a private chef cook her meals, ordered a case of special water that wasn't even sold locally, and kept people away from her as much as possible. She wanted to be there only out of duty or some obligation to the church, it seemed, not because she really wanted to be there and engage the staff and students, except during the graduation ceremony. Although very distant, she was quiet and polite and didn't come across as arrogant.

Priscilla's presence definitely helped the press coverage of the event, though. Right before a scheduled media interview in McAlester, she came to my office with her Celebrity Centre escort and we had a chance to talk for a bit before heading down. She had already done a brief phone interview with an AP writer from Oklahoma City, and then the in-person interviews came with the McAlester Radio newsman and the News-Capital representatives. Presley was quoted as saying she believed Elvis would still be alive today if he had been to a program like Narconon Arrowhead. It was a golden quote and the PR value did wind up being more valuable than the extra cost of her being there. She also spoke at the event on Saturday night.

In addition to serving up possibly an interview chance of a lifetime with Priscilla to the local paper (the senior editor was an Elvis fan), I had come up with the idea to do two things at the event. One was to select a few local organizations to present $1,000 donation checks to in front of the crowd to demonstrate our support of the community, and the other was to present an award to then-publisher of the News-Capital Chris White for his dedication to highlighting drug education and treatment in the media.

In addition to the grantees receiving checks, Priscilla Presley and Chris White coming up on stage, we also had Oklahoma Senator Richard Lerblance (who replaced Gene Stipe) and local District Attorney Chris Wilson give speeches. Opening the ceremony were Native American dancers and color guard (the facility is in Choctaw Nation), Rev. James McLaughlin sang the National Anthem and delivered an invocation and Donna Woods from the Oklahoma Citizen Advocates for Recovery and Treatment Association (OCARTA) spoke on behalf of her organization.

One by one, every person brought up on stage at the event that Saturday night in September sang praises for Narconon Arrowhead, and I don't know if the acceptance of the organization had ever been higher than that time period between 2001 and 2005.

There was also a great reflection nationally. I used to write articles and press releases and we would send them out to newspapers, magazines and websites throughout the country. The press archives for 2003 alone showed more than 25,000 column inches of positive press that we had garnered throughout the country - for free. Hundreds of publications across the nation spanning all 50 states published articles.

Auditing at Narconon and then going to LA

Narconon encouraged staff to become Scientologists and to get on the Bridge, though it was not a requirement. However, it was widely known that all of the senior executives - the people who really called the shots - were Scientologists and that there was little room for advancement unless you were.

There were many ways that Narconon Arrowhead paid money for Scientology services for staff. Often times it would be sending people to a church and paying for all or part of the cost, which ranges in the thousands. In fact, one regular 12 1/2 hr intensive of auditing is $2,000 for a staff member (usually more, but we got half price off the full rate) at what are called Class V churches.

These Orgs can audit a person up to the state of Clear, but no further, and include places like Atlanta, Dallas, Kansas City, Tampa and even CC Int.

The half-price rates go up from there. At American St. Hill Organization (ASHO) they were $2,600 each, at the Advanced Organization Los Angeles (AOLA) they were $2,800 each and down at Flag they reached from $3,400 all the way up to $4,500. Remember, these are half off the full price. Scientology loves packages, so they discount them down if you're in IAS member, or if you buy in bulk, but they would never be as low as what we got them for as staff members. The only services that I'm aware of that are not discounted are something called the L Rundowns, which were a series of high-level processes that cost $12,000 per intensive. That's right, basically $1,000 per hour, yet they still call these donations.

In addition to sending people to various Orgs for auditing and training, Arrowhead would also pay to have auditors come out and have sessions with staff members, as I mentioned previously. Usually there were about two at a time, and the average pay for them was $2,000 per week, sometimes more and sometimes less. It was a good deal for the auditors because they wouldn't have any expenses and have some guaranteed income for a while, but it was an even better deal for Arrowhead, because they could send multiple staff members in session each week but only have to pay for one intensive per auditor. Names of auditors over the years included Mary Rieser, Richie Almstead, Rory Tate, Marty Gutman and others.

There was a time when there were 50 or more staff wanting to get into the line-up for auditing, with others who could only go to Orgs for services. We had church-trained case supervisors who worked to oversee both the program delivery to students as well as the staff auditing. Case supervisors included Les Moore, Roy Brock and Joe and Claire Pinelli.

An entire cabin was dedicated as the Arrowhead Hubbard Guidance Center (An HGC in an org is where the auditing is delivered), complete with a new deck on it.

At one point the church organization in charge of field auditors called the International Hubbard Ecclesiastical League of Pastors

(IHELP) told Arrowhead that they could not employ auditors unless they were a church, and if not then they had to pay the auditors standard rates because IHELP wanted its cut. All field auditors are required to be members of IHELP, report their statistics and pay them a portion of their income, like a franchise fee. Other terms also come to mind though, like racket.

We didn't want to comply with that so all auditing provided on campus stopped for a period of time and staff just went to Orgs instead. A later solution came when a field auditor group called Infinity Management from Austin, TX started coming up twice a month. They were run by Lee Crosley and his family.

Since my scheduling was sometimes unpredictable with meetings, I stopped getting sporadic auditing sessions at Arrowhead and planned a trip out to CC Int in November of 2003 for a couple weeks. I drove out and stayed at a nearby motel rather than paying room rates at the Celebrity Centre's Manor Hotel.

While I was there I was asked by Maria Ferrara to meet with her and talk to someone about Narconon. I went to the President's office and she introduced me to Matt Sorum, the drummer formerly with Guns 'N Roses. A female Scientologist had befriended him. He was then a part of Velvet Revolver, whose singer was former Stone Temple Pilots frontman Scott Weiland. It was no secret Scott had some substance abuse issues, and the woman with Matt and Maria were trying to convince him to get Scott to come to Narconon Arrowhead. I told him about the program and he was very nice and said that he and other members of the band had all used different methods to beat their addictions and he just wanted to find something that would work for Scott. The meeting didn't last very long, but I left him with a brochure and he said he'd give it to Scott's attorney. He never wound up coming to Arrowhead, or any other Narconon that I'm aware of, so the meeting was futile. It was just another example of how the Celebrity Centre was used to recruit artists for various Scientology groups.

The auditor assigned to me was Marcilleno Manzano and he had a very heavy Italian accent. It made it difficult to understand some of the questions he asked and it really affected the auditing sessions. First I had to finish up my Grade I on the Bridge, which also includes doing some more Objectives. I was quite irritated because it seemed so elementary. After all, I still believed at that time that I had gone beyond the state of Clear on the Bridge and that the lower Grades were beneath me.

I was pretty upset and asked to see someone to talk about it, especially since Mike Gosselin had been pronounced Clear there recently although he hadn't had any auditing in many years prior to that. It seemed to me and others that I worked with that he had much more visible "case" attitude problems and seemingly irrational thoughts. A Clear was supposed to not have irrational thoughts (no "held down sevens" as Hubbard called it) and I was this young prodigy in the Narconon world, by god. Well, that was my thought process at the time, anyway. Scientology definitely feeds the self-important status-hungry ego side of people.

I wound up getting in an argument with a woman from the Qualifications Division there and we didn't make any progress, so I just decided to shut up and go back in session. I quickly completed Grade I after that.

Then I started doing Grade II, which is all about overts and withholds, and includes the infamous Johannesburg Confessional. The Joburg, as it's called, was designed by L. Ron Hubbard in 1961 and includes a list of questions trying to find out your past crimes. It even includes ridiculous things such as "Have you ever done any illicit diamond buying?", "Have you ever been a spy for an organization?", "Have you ever been a newspaper reporter?", "How do you feel about being controlled?" and "Have you ever slept with a member of a race of another color?" among the nearly 100 questions.

It was grueling. Not so much for the questions themselves, but because I had a hard time understanding him and the e-meter wouldn't react properly so he would keep checking the questions if the needle didn't float. We went on for days and days and days going over these, only to usually find out that we should have gone on to the next question hours earlier in many cases. It was a major waste of time, and money.

Needless to say I didn't complete it in time and had to leave, which is a big no-no in Scientology. We had to at least get to a good ending point, at which we had to do something called end rudiments, which is making sure that I didn't leave anything out and that nothing got missed. One of the questions that is part of doing end rudiments is "Have you told all?" Indeed I had and I was ready to get the hell out of there. I was finally given approval to leave, though with serious reluctance.

I drove back to Oklahoma ready for the Holidays. I was also ready to get back to work, which seemed more like a break than my break to go in session at CC Int.

A couple weeks later during the Scientology New Year's Event, church President Heber Jentzsch gave the Narconon Arrowhead update. The speech included the mention that I had been elected to the Executive Board of OSASA, but made it appear as if Narconon was taking the lead in the state, and they had even altered an image of me speaking at the anniversary event and placed an OSASA sign on the podium. It presented a false picture that somehow I was addressing a large audience as the leader of OSASA, which simply wasn't true. That same picture was then featured in the annual International Scientology News magazine, with the headline "Narconon Takes the Lead". It was more propaganda to present a false image to parishioners and extract more money out of them.

Arrowhead Strategy

The legal and legislative landscape was still uncertain at the end of 2003. Gary Smith typed up several targets for PR strategy in the upcoming year. In this, one of them was to "Get wording for the bill that will be going through to correct our licensing situation in Oklahoma by Jan 15th latest."

After pussyfooting around for months on approaching the Dept. of Mental Health, who had repeatedly stated they didn't want to fight and would work with us, OSA still wouldn't allow it and had to coordinate and entire plan. They had hired a former ODMHSAS staff member and Board Member at 12 & 12 treatment center in Tulsa, Sydney Kriter, to do a mock inspection of the facility and consult on the current regulations in the state. She was well known in the state's substance abuse and mental health field and a friend of mine from OSASA.

There was also still no formal outcome study done and Smith wanted to use Dr. Emery Johnson to try and solicit help doing an internal one that could be presented to people, which he listed as another target. Emery was a former Assistant Surgeon General and was on an advisory board for the Robert Wood Johnson Foundation. He had been introduced to Narconon through attorney Sandy McNabb back from the days when they worked with the Bureau of Indian Affairs together in some capacity.

Since the IAS wasn't going to give another grant to Arrowhead for the expansion plans, they had engaged in a feasibility study to see if we could raise the money through alumni and local contacts. Additional targets Gary wrote down included "Get fundraising packs put together for alumni, local and state business people," and "Work out meetings and presentations to Oklahoma's top 20 business people. Wanda Bass, Bank of OK, the banking family Peggy knows in Checotah, etc."

He also wanted updated legislative briefing packs put together, since the last ones had gone out back in May of that year. All of these actions were taking place, in addition to the hiring of a lobbyist and David Riggs to gear up for some imaginary battle. All they had to do was simply decide to cooperate with the state, but they would rather use up tons of time and resources to bend the rules rather than comply like everyone else.

As another move of manipulation, Gary and Vicki plotted to hire someone connected to legislative aide Connie Johnson. The woman had already been through the program for free to gain favor, and then they wanted her put in my office because of her connection to the Oklahoma legislature. The woman wound up leaving after only a few months, but Connie Johnson also wound up being elected as a State Senator soon after that and I'm sure the favor didn't go unnoticed.

Arrowhead was so concerned about its licensing situation that Gary Smith issued a series of steps at the end of January in 2004 that were to be followed that covered multiple avenues such as introducing new legislation, support from elected officials, determining opinion leaders (OLs – people who have influence over others in their circles) to be used as supporters, and finding ways to gain protection in the state.

Some of these instructions included working with the lobbyist and lawyers on promoting the economic benefits of having Arrowhead in the state and its expansion plans, neutralizing ODMHSAS Board member Dwight Holden and Deputy Commissioner Ben Brown as well as finding out exactly which legislators were supportive and which ones weren't. It also had instructions for me to work with OSASA on getting support from other treatment centers as well as trying to get Narconon's counselor certifications accepted in the state. It went on from there. The whole idea was to find any and all support from as many areas and high positions as possible.

It was getting pretty heavy, and I was getting pretty sick of it all because it was out of my control and I was just getting ordered around for OSA's grand master plan of attack they conjured up with Mike St. Amand and Gary Smith.

7 STEPPING DOWN AS PRESIDENT

    After getting back from LA, I spent the next several weeks trudging through work. It wasn't going well at all. I was getting cross orders from Gary, Clark, Rena and CC Int, Erica was very jealous and didn't want me to be President and we fought frequently, and I was generally sick of the whole scene. I had to get out of there. I wrote something to Rena about how frustrated I was about everything and stated, "...I simply feel trapped here and need the freedom to create as an individual..."

    I had requested to be transferred to the Narconon in Georgia. No dice. Instead I was ordered back out to CC Int. I thought it was to finish my Grade II, but what really happened was I was put in with their Senior Sec Checker Colleen Weigand. She was their little bulldog who was supposed to dig in and find out all my overts. They were certain that I must have done something wrong to want to leave my position, as Hubbard wrote that the only reason a person blows (leaves) is because of his or her own overts. What awfully presumptuous and high-horse statement that is – to assume that the group is always right and the individual is always wrong for wanting to leave.

    We went through more than a solid week of intense sec checks. She would turn in reports at the end of each day on any little thing found out, and these were compiled. Sometimes we would sit for hours on the same question. I was so angry about having to be there in the first place and yet completely stuck, because if I left then it would only "prove" to them they were right. I found myself yelling at Colleen because the entrapment I felt was directed at her since she was the only one there. Afterward, she would simply say, "Are you done? I'll repeat the question…"

The questions were very broad, such as "What have you done that (insert name) doesn't know about?" They wanted to know anything and everything that I might possibly have done to cause me not want to be the President anymore. The Case Supervisor at CC Int got input from Narconon on what to ask me, as well as going through my auditing folders to look for possible trouble areas. As soon as I finished one set of questions, it would go back up and come back with more questions.

In between sec check sessions I would go over to Narconon Int's office or ABLE Int's office and do menial work. I did things such as wash dishes in the break room, sweep off a patio, wash off multiple sets of vertical blinds and re-hang them, move furniture at Narconon International. I also scrubbed the front retaining wall across the street at ABLE, trimmed the hedges on the wall, scrubbed the side of the building where there were stains and swept the front and back courtyards. I had been brought back to an apartment complex behind ABLE that the church had paid for to help clear it out and bring things to a dumpster before it was renovated, but that only lasted for a little bit as they decided they didn't have liability insurance to cover me if I was injured.

I went back and forth between my hotel, CC Int, Narconon Int, and ABLE Int, doing whatever I was asked to do. I was also given multiple LRH references to read as study orders, and would do so in the basement of CC Int and the basement of ABLE Int. At one point, I had to do something called Method 9 word-clearing on entire references and chapters in the Introduction to Scientology Ethics book. That is where you have to read aloud to another person who follows along. Any time there is an imperfection in the reading, mispronunciation of a word, substitution of a word or hesitation on a word, you are stopped by the coach and you have to look up the word, read all the definitions and give examples for each and then read the derivation. After the word was cleared, you have to go back and re-read the section just before you messed up, and then continue on from there. It takes many hours to M-9 references by Hubbard, as his writing style was very odd and didn't flow like most books or sets of instructions. They were also written in earlier decades where some words aren't heard much now but were used more frequently back then.

My coach for the M-9 was Bob Adams, who was still posted as the VP of ABLE at the time. I will say that Bob Adams is a very kind and patient man. His personal interest seemed to be for me to do well, and it was much less involved with my job, which I appreciated since the others were all more concerned with the latter.

Many days I would go and sit downstairs at the public MAA's office in the basement of CC Int and just wait for the next thing. MAA stands for Master at Arms, and is the Sea Org equivalent of an ethics officer. Usually I would leave and tell them to call me when they had something. One day I went to talk to the young, red-headed girl who was my MAA and said, "I don't get it. Am I being treated like a paying public, or a staff member? If I'm public, then I've actually done nothing wrong. If I'm being treated like a staff member, then why the hell am I even down here doing this?"

"I don't actually know," she said. "I am not really sure what's happening. We're getting directions from ABLE, Narconon, the C/S and the President's office here."

Well, that confirmed exactly what I was talking about. The lines were so crossed that nobody knew who was actually responsible. They all wanted to be, but in the end, nobody really wanted to be. So I left again and just told her to call me when she heard something.

During this time Clark had asked me to write up what I thought was really wrong with the President's office at Arrowhead, so I gave my honest evaluation of the scene. In a communication dated March 31, 2004, I stated that there was a familial hierarchy that governs Narconon Arrowhead. This included Gary Smith, his wife and her daughter Rebecca. It also included Mike and Maureen St. Amand and Mike and Kathy Gosselin. These people sat atop the organization for years and controlled all of the decisions and finances, yet when better staff members came along who produced more income or better results, they stifled the improvements by tightening the reigns.

I also mentioned the cross purposes of my position and how much of what NN Int, ABLE, and other various church organizations in LA ordered me to do was actually looked upon by staff at Arrowhead as being a burden, including Gary Smith. I explained how his wife was posted as my Aide yet any disagreement she had with what I was doing she would simply go tell her husband. She would also use Gary to do her little vanity projects that only she really thought were important.

I noted that the necessity for a medical detox facility was vital to the long-term survival of the organization, but that people at Narconon Int, ABLE and the church were prohibiting that out of some false notion that Hubbard's withdrawal methods could actually handle any drug situation.

Another point of contention was that there was much more scrutiny placed on Arrowhead since the Scientology world was focused on it that other Narconon centers didn't have to adhere to. Narconon Int failed to control many of the other centers despite their obligation to do so.

A couple of days later Gary Smith was in town for a briefing with ABLE and OSA regarding the state certification problem. He met me for dinner and pulled out the report that I had written for Clark. I thought I was writing it only for Clark and was very frank in it, so it was a bit of a shock that he gave it to him. Nothing in Scientology is truly confidential – it is always shared with someone and used against you at some point.

Gary looked at me and said, "This is pretty fucked up, man. I get it that you feel stuck in between all of this, but these people at Arrowhead are the reasons why it still exists, whether you see it or not. Do you still feel this way?"

Pausing, I finally replied, "Yes, I do."

Then Gary retorted, "Well maybe this isn't your group then. I think you should take some time to really assess the good deal you had going, but I don't think you can get that back now."

Gary left shortly after that. The part about it not really being my group seemed to stick with me. It has ever since. I thought I was doing good things for a good group of people trying to help others. That may be what it appears to be on the surface, but that absolutely isn't what is really going on underneath it all. Most of the people who work at Narconon centers believe they are helping people and are unaware of what happens at the executive levels and higher echelons of the Scientology corporations.

By then I had been there a month already, and my hotel told me I had to check out for at least one night, so I went to a Days Inn down off Vermont Avenue instead. It was a couple miles, and I literally walked with my suitcase and other bag the entire way, drenched in sweat. This hotel was around the corner from the PAC base where ASHO, AOLA, the LA Org and many regional offices were located.

I soon began complaining more at CC Int about why there was such a hold-up. I had done everything they asked up to that point, including studying, the sec checks and manual labor. I was finally called in one day and told I was no longer eligible for services at CC Int, and that I was being transferred to ASHO, but that I needed to go have a release of liability waiver signed and notarized as well in order to complete it.

After several days of the people at ASHO studying my folders to get caught up on everything, I finally got back in with one of their auditors to resume my sec check. I was asked a couple of questions about some incident or time period, and came up clean. A few days later I was called back in again and asked one or two more questions, which also came up clean. My folders went back in to be reviewed again, and a few more days later I was finally deemed complete. Normally in Scientology you have to attest to the completion of any auditing or training action, but since this was such an odd situation with many chefs in the kitchen, there wasn't anything for me to attest to, I was just allowed to go back on to finish my Grade II confessional after I completed lower conditions and made up damage to them.

To wrap the whole thing up, I met with Clark again at his office. I proposed that I take a leave of absence to "handle my lower condition" with the group. Clark had typed up an Urgent Directive that stated I was no longer qualified to be the President and could resume being a staff member when I completed my repair program. We agreed that I would go to the Atlanta Org and complete the Student Hat Course (a study course that is a prerequisite to any major course in Scientology), the PTS/SP Course and complete my Grade II auditing.

Finally, after being stuck there for seven weeks, I was able to leave with agreed-upon terms. I was just happy to not be the President of Arrowhead anymore, to be able to spend some time in GA and to be away from LA.

My Leave of Absence

Before heading to Georgia, there were several things I had to wrap up and turn over to others. I wrote updates for Gary, Vicki, Derry and Peggy on all of the things I was involved with prior to going to LA. At my desk there was a message that Erika Christensen had called. It said she was researching a role and needed information on methamphetamine. I called her and caught her right before she was boarding a plane. I told her that I would have one of our other staff members call her back to provide any information she needed.

I had worked it out to be able to do interventions for Arrowhead while I took my leave of absence, where family members pay for assistance getting someone into the program. I wasn't receiving any staff pay, but was responsible for paying for my training and auditing in Atlanta, which cost several thousand dollars. I was also going to continue writing web articles, content pages and news releases for them for free.

Before I left for Georgia, Erica and I split our bank accounts. I later found out that while I was in LA, Gary Smith and her immediate boss Derry Hallmark (someone who I thought was a friend) were afraid that she would leave too, and were telling her that people who leave Narconon don't usually make it. They said that I was unstable and would probably relapse to drug use and instilled even more fear in her so that she would cling tightly to the group. Scientology activities thrive on keeping members close like that, making them think that the group's survival is the most important thing and therefore sacrifices have to be made. It also manipulates people into thinking that they can't survive without the group.

So I drove back East to Georgia and began taking my courses. Most days I was in the course room I was the only person in there who wasn't a staff member during the weekdays. On evenings and weekends a few people would trickle in, but that was about the extent of participation, in a metropolitan area reaching more than four million people.

Over the next few months I spent time driving back to Oklahoma every other week, doing interventions for Arrowhead, and spending time at the Atlanta Org. I finished the last few questions on my Grade II, then completed Grade III and did almost all of Grade IV. I also completed both of my courses, and in September decided it was time to finally go back to Arrowhead for good.

Back to Arrowhead

When I first got back to officially finish the remainder of my staff contract, they were in the middle of having their anniversary event again. Gary asked me to stay out of the way and out of site to not cause any confusion for people or for them to ask questions, particularly people in the community who noticed I was gone. I think he was also frustrated that he wound up having to be involved in planning and carrying out the event.

I had taken on a much lower position toward the bottom of Division 6A, which was for promoting to get new people to reach in for more information about our services. I started working on the websites in close coordination with Derry. When I started back the new contacts (called reaches) from the Internet were down below 200 per week. Over time they steadily kept rising and went up to over 225 per week. Derry then wanted to add a database of state and city pages to the main site like he had seen at some other centers, which would generate many thousands of new pages. I wrote the content for the main state pages and then two outside sources, both Scientologists, were hired to do the programming and installation. Once Google indexed all of the new pages we shot back up to over 1,000 Internet reaches per week within a month.

I was also helping out by writing news articles and press releases again, as well as doing radio interviews. The labor laws had changed in Oklahoma and you had to pay someone at least $450 per week if they were going to be salaried, otherwise they had to be paid by the hour. Since I was back down in a lower spot, I would hit my 40 hours per week easily and would wind up being able to take extra afternoons and weekend time off. Overtime had to be approved in advance and usually was restricted to people working in the program delivery areas. I was making next to nothing, but happy about the low level of stress.

The Counselor Certification Front

Around this same time there was a big push to get as many people to become Certified Chemical Dependency Counselors (CCDCs) as possible. This was a counselor certification through an organization called the National Association of Forensic Counselors (NAFC). A few people had gotten theirs years earlier, such as Gary Smith, and they allowed non-degree people to get certified if they worked in the field long enough. It was never a certification that has been an accepted credential in the state of Oklahoma though, and was done primarily for PR purposes to say that we had X number of certified counselors on staff. As incentive, anyone who was able to get certified received an extra $100 per week bonus. I was short on money and really wanted that bonus. We had already done one round several months earlier when I was President, adding 19 new certifications, and were ready for more due to staff turnover and more people being eligible.

Kent McGregor had set up a line with the NAFC to proctor the exams and get people certified. He was the former surveyor for the Commission on Accreditation for Rehabilitation Facilities (CARF) who had been to Chilocco in 1991 that was used to end the feud with the state, as was mentioned before. He met his wife

Jette (pronounced Yetta) when she was working at Chilocco back then and he has been involved with Narconon ever since, mostly as an FSM and consultant.

So anyone who could come close to the minimum requirements of hours of practical experience and/or educational background was somehow "qualified" to apply for a CCDC and take the test. Gary, Kent and others signed off on all of the applications as having verified the correctness of the qualifications and documented hours to recommend each individual. Since I had been there long enough by then, I was also allowed to apply for certification.

Once approved, all we had to do was pass a test. The test was primarily based on one book, so all staff members preparing for the test were to study that book and were told to try and forget the information afterward since most didn't apply to what Narconon did. Kent also supplied a cheat sheet with what he thought the answers were. I never read the book and instead read over that cheat sheet. I had always been pretty decent at taking tests, especially multiple choice questions, and figured I'd wing it if his answers were wrong.

Once it was approved, we went into the staff course room and took the test under Kent's supervision. I zipped through, guessing on down. Kent was careful not to directly give answers during the test, but asked people if they had any questions on any of them and gave hints to a few that were there. Once all the tests were sealed and turned in, they were sent off with a big check to the NAFC to have the exams graded. A few weeks later I joined a couple dozen co-workers as having the bullshit distinction of being a Certified Chemical Dependency Counselor, complete with a certificate from the National Board of Addiction Examiners (a division of the NAFC). I was just happy to get the extra bonus each week, since that made up for my lack of overtime hours. Although I admit I kept up the charade for years, I finally dropped my CCDC status, as recognition of the truth that it meant basically nothing in the field of addiction counseling and that I wasn't qualified to be considered a certified counselor.

Kent then went on to work with other Narconon centers and Narconon International to get more staff members certified. To this day many of them promote their CCDCs still as having some sort of validity, and the NAFC continues to accept the $85 per person renewal fees each year.

Cruise to the Rescue

In 2004, JT Daily was the Director of Drug Education for Narconon Arrowhead and had been in New York delivering drug education to classes that were touring through the DEA's exhibit in Times Square. Narconon Arrowhead had been featured in the Target America exhibit because staff member DannaSue Pruett submitted material that was accepted, and then helped book JT out there. The museum intended to highlight the notion that the opium poppy trade in Afghanistan was helping to fund terrorist activities.

Somehow Narconon shared drug education space with another rehab program called Daytop to talk to kids, as busloads of students from around the area were brought in to tour the exhibit as part of Red Ribbon Week in late October. JT was out there for several weeks, and had formed a friendship with Amy Bloustine, who was a demand reduction coordinator for the exhibit. As usual, once Narconon International and ABLE found out about it, they wanted to spin it into their own PR. Narconon East US Executive Director Yvonne Rogers was dispatched out there to take pictures and try and "safepoint" Ms. Bloustine and other DEA personnel to take advantage of in the future. Yvonne and Narconon International nearly blew it completely due to their overzealous nature and PR-hungry blunders, but JT's natural likeability and connection to Amy withstood the additional influence.

During this time Gary Smith got a call from CC Int to fly immediately to New York City. Tom Cruise was filming War of the Worlds near there and wanted Gary to come along and help talk about Narconon to someone on the set. Since JT Daily was in New York already, Gary mentioned having him be present as well. Gary and JT were picked up by a helicopter in NYC and brought to the set, where they met with Tom in a private trailer and spoke with him and the other person in secrecy. Both Gary and JT were forced to sign bonded agreements to not identify who they were meeting with. Looking back, this is very ironic since the church repeatedly violated the confidentiality of Narconon clients, but I guess whatever Tom Cruise wants, the church delivers.

Also on the set was a bright yellow Scientology Volunteer Minister tent, where Tom had made introductory Scientology material available for anyone who wanted to find out more. He also had the VMs deliver Scientology assists to others as an attempt to offer aid to people who were injured or fatigued.

Upon returning home from the New York trip, Tom Cruise actually had ordered that Gary Smith get corrected on his Hard Sell tactics regarding Narconon being the best program on the planet, and something called a cram order was issued to him from CC Int that he had to comply with.

Following the high of having Narconon drug education in the DEA museum, it received a huge blow when the San Francisco Chronicle reported in August of 2004 that Narconon was banned from delivering presentations in their public schools. It would eventually be reviewed by the California State Board of Education and removed from the entire system the following year.

Cruise Receives His Freedom Medal

In late October of 2004, Tom Cruise was awarded a special medal from David Miscavige called the IAS Freedom Medal of Valor. Gary Smith told me that Cruise wanted to win a Freedom Medal more than he wanted to win an Oscar. The DVD for the event was sent to Arrowhead and was shown in the staff course room for all those who wished to watch it.

Even as a dedicated Scientologist myself at the time, I found the (now infamous) interview with Cruise in his black turtleneck talking about what it means to be a Scientologist to be quite over the top and embarrassing. His uncomfortable and somewhat uncontrollable laughing at inappropriate times is off-putting and is so awkward that it seems better suited for a scene with Dwight Schrute in The Office.

What is not fully known or understood to the outside world, there are additional duties that IAS Freedom Medal winners are given each year at the annual event in England. They have bonded meetings to discuss the goals of Scientology and then set individual targets to accomplish for the upcoming year. They fall within the realm of the direction Miscavige is taking the organization combined with their spheres of influence. It is expected above and beyond what "normal" Scientologists do, as their efforts to spread the subject and forward the aims of the group are what got them awarded the medal in the first place.

Since Tom Cruise has a huge circle of influence nationally and internationally, his goals undoubtedly included recruiting other high-profile and powerful people into Scientology. This is how stories like his courtship of Will Smith, David Beckham, Dan Snyder (Washington Redskins owner and former investor in United Artists) and others surface. I don't know if Beckham or Snyder have ever had any dealings with Scientology, but it is widely known that Will Smith at least wound up opening a school that uses Hubbard's Study Tech. Whether or not he is considered by them a friend and he is nice to them, Tom Cruise is used just like every other Scientologist to recruit new members, especially members with money and influence. The title of the landmark 1991 Time magazine cover story by Richard Behar, "The Thriving Cult of Greed and Power", couldn't have been a more succinct description.

Another function of Freedom Medal winners is to nominate other people for consideration of winning a medal in the future. Bobby Wiggins told me that he had nominated me in 2003, but that I just hadn't been around long enough yet to be considered. Knowing how much pressure average Scientologists get to recruit and get money, I can't imagine the pressure put on IAS Freedom Medal winners and am thankful that I wasn't ever seriously considered. In addition, having worked closely with four winners during my time with Narconon (Rena, Gary, Bobby and Jeannie), I'd hate to think that I would have developed an even greater depth of judgmental tone toward the rest of the world in believing that only we really knew what was best for mankind.

Taking on More Roles Again

Kelly Preston helped secure money to open a Narconon in Hawaii, starting with drug education. I was told that it was a donation from Barbara Cox Anthony, who was a resident of Hawaii and formerly the richest person in the state, who was used to fund the operation in the beginning. Kelly Preston is a native of Hawaii and had been out for a visit to Arrowhead in late 2004.

Rena and Clark wanted me to go out to Hawaii for some PR work and drug education. Gary Smith pulled me into his office and told me that I was requested to go out to Hawaii for the project and told me it was right up my alley. I said I had to think about it because they told me it was going to be for two or three weeks, but I knew that chances were likely that it was going to be much longer than that.

I was able to think quickly and ask Bobby Newman if he was interested in going. By then he had worked up to running Division 6C, which was over community relations, drug education and the Field Staff Members (FSMs). I told him I could help cover his stuff while he was gone. I called Gary back and told him I didn't want to go and asked if Bobby Newman could go instead. He was able to get approval from Rena and Clark and wound up flying out the next day.

Not long after Bobby arrived in Hawaii, the state department of education had reviewed the decision in California and wouldn't allow Narconon drug prevention in their public schools either, so Bobby Newman was left to work only with private schools for a while.

Meanwhile, things were still booming at Arrowhead in early 2005. We had a huge machine that was repeatedly churning out $300,000 per week in revenue for several months, hitting as high as nearly half a million one week. After all, money was the main focus. Phil Hart would call in almost daily from Narconon Int and ask what the Gross Income (GI) was so far for the week. He would also want to know what the projected week-ending GI total would be as well as how much money was already lined up for the next week. This can be verified by anyone who worked on the 800 receptionist position at Arrowhead for any length of time.

Included in all of the promotion that we did were the radio shows. A woman named Sharon Nederlander was posted as the person who called the radio stations to book the interviews, and at one time we were doing well over 20 radio shows per week throughout the country. They would be at different times of the day and lasted anywhere from 3 minutes to an hour in length. Sharon had booked more radio shows than anyone in the past, and the reaches from the radio went from about five per week to over 100 due to her efforts.

One day Sharon didn't show up for work. Former president Michael Anzalone had come back on staff by then in a different position and was sent out to find her. He was in contact with her family and was able to trace her to a hotel. When he arrived he found that she had died from alcohol poisoning alone in her hotel room. While several of us found out, it was kept very hush-hush for the most part amongst the staff and sort of swept under the rug, but it was still very disturbing. What also set me on edge was that Michael began using a Louis Vuitton leather portfolio of Sharon's that he claimed the family said he could keep.

Anzalone had married a young staff member named Amanda Myers. She had worked in Division 6A as well and he was often up in the other building. Something still didn't seem right with him, and both Derry and I agreed there was more going on underneath. It was eventually found out that Michael had gone back to using painkillers again and was kicked off staff for a second time. Amanda eventually left as well.

Soon I found myself getting spread a little thin since I was covering for Bobby and it was apparent he wasn't coming back. Within a short period of time I was the head of both Divisions 6A and 6C.

The concept of an FSM is of course from the church and there are many policies in Scientology and Narconon that talk about FSMs, including what their job is and how they get paid. Hubbard said the job of an FSM is to successfully use his Dissemination

Drill, which includes four steps: Contact, Handle, Salvage and Bring to Understanding.

Part of the Salvage step is called finding the ruin of the person. This is a fundamental tool used to sell Scientology services - find out what is ruining their lives, especially what they personally think to be the biggest problem or set of problems. You then talk to them about how a particular aspect of the program or steps will help them solve those problems specifically. Whether or not there is any success at first, the trick is that they then try and find another ruin and sell you more services, products or materials. It is a sales scheme, but when you're a True Believer you think that you're doing the best thing for that person.

Since I had been working on Arrowhead's websites, I also started to help some FSMs with their websites because if their reaches were increasing then our income would go up, too. At the time we were paying out an average of $15,000 to $20,000 per week in commissions to FSMs. The highest amount paid in commissions back then was $25,000 in one week.

Despite generating more than a thousand leads directly to the center, roughly three quarters of the people who actually enrolled in the program at Arrowhead somehow had been in touch with an FSM. This fabricated third party endorsement was part of the overall scheme. There would often be times where people would contact the facility directly, be unsure about it and keep researching, only to come across an FSM website and call the number. After speaking to an FSM they then got re-routed back to the facility and closed to come to the program.

Cruise Brings Katie Holmes for a Visit

In the early fall of 2005, we had gotten word that Tom Cruise was coming for another visit, but this time a fully public one. In tow was the typical entourage including church representatives and a reporter from a German magazine. Oh, and Katie Holmes. Unbeknownst to anyone there at the time, Katie was already pregnant since Suri was born in April of the next year.

It was an odd dual display. On one hand Tom seemed to be showing off Arrowhead to Katie and the reporter, and on the other hand he seemed to be showing off Katie in front of everyone. This time rather than making all the staff and students huddle in certain areas, few people knew they were coming and so they were going about their business. They were taken totally by surprise as the crew quietly opened the doors to the course rooms, the sauna, the cafeteria, and other parts of the building.

My wife and I were selected to be two of the staff on hand for the tour. One reason was because we were executives, but also because we presented ourselves well to the newly-engaged couple. Katie is a year younger than me and a year older than Erica.

At one point we were standing in the lobby, face to face with the couple. Katie was doe eyed and towered over Tom while she heard shortened versions of our stories. After Erica finished speaking Tom said, "Wow, very well done!" and Katie exclaimed, "That is amazing, I never would have guessed you were addicted to heroin."

Just moments after that Tom turned to Katie and started kissing her. It wasn't just a peck, but wasn't a full-on make out session either, more like an awkwardly long embrace that was only made even more uncomfortable by the fact that at least a dozen people were standing around watching. It was a completely inappropriate time to lip lock like that. She seemed taken aback by it as well and it was definitely not the level of comfort that one might expect from people who were engaged to be married.

On the way out the door Tom went up and tapped Erica on the shoulder. She turned around and she spoke with him and Katie again for a few more minutes about the program before saying their goodbyes. Right after that, one of the Sea Org members there with the entourage who was a woman went up to Erica and said, "Can you believe that Tom Cruise just tapped you on the shoulder and was talking to you?!" Sea Org members treat Cruise like a god.

Working on My Transition

When I was younger I wanted to work in film and television. I had fallen for basically a vanity agency in Atlanta when I was 19, took some acting classes through them and went on a few auditions. Surprisingly, I landed a lead role in a small independent film called Mama's Boy that was being produced locally, however production halted two weeks before the scheduled shooting time and the film never got made, to my knowledge. For all I know it could have been a total sham, but it was exciting nonetheless.

Ever since then I really wanted to be involved in the industry somehow, and one night after work I was thinking about how there really weren't any active Narconon spokespeople. Kirstie Alley hadn't done much for Narconon in years, and Priscilla seemed like she was doing it out of obligation to the church and not a passion. Others had various involvements or mentions but that was it.

I drew up a plan to write a film script and cast it primarily with actual Narconon graduates and staff members from around the country. It could be funded and produced with Scientology connections, and the money made from the film would go toward expansion of the network while the stars of the film became recognizable celebrities themselves and would want to constantly promote Narconon. I just wanted to write it and be involved in the production.

Yes, I realize now how crazy it sounds that I wanted to do that, but I was dead set carrying forward. I started writing the script, which was basically about drugs and addiction and actually promoted Narconon within it. It took me a while, but I finished it after several months and began looking for any kind of support, which included emailing Scientologists who weren't necessarily big celebrities but did routinely work in the business.

I finally got a response from Jim Meskimen, who is a character actor in film and has done many commercials and a lot of voiceover work. I had also met him at a birthday party for Clark Carr in LA previously. Jim told me about Eric Sherman, who is a film professor at the Art Center in Pasadena and also a film consultant for producers, directors and actors. I called him and set up a time to go see him shortly after my contract was up. I was excited because it seemed like I was on my way to doing something.

One of the scenes I wrote included a psychiatrist at a treatment facility giving prescription drugs to female patients in exchange for sexual favors. Scientologists hate psychiatry and I believed in their propaganda. I still believe personally in exploring more natural solutions first, but no longer condemn psychiatry or psychology en masse like Scientology does. Little did I know at the time, but the scenario of giving drugs to patients for sex is actually more likely to happen at a Narconon center than at traditional treatment programs.

The Concept of a Celebrity Narconon

There was a lot of talk about creating a separate facility at Arrowhead or elsewhere for celebrities to be able to do the program in private. One day in late 2005 I got a call from Simon Hogarth, who was the Narconon representative for ABLE. He told me that ABLE was going to set up a celebrity Narconon at a home in the Hollywood Hills and that ABLE would be in charge of it, not Narconon International. He said a home had already been chosen and he asked me to come immediately to help set it up and be the Executive Director.

I already had my mind set on making my film, and told him about that. He tried to talk me out of it and basically said it was a long shot and I was too much of a dreamer, but that running the celebrity Narconon would give me a greater chance of making something like that happen. I didn't buy it though, and asked what would happen with Erica. He told me she'd have to stay behind in Oklahoma, but that after she finished her staff contract she could join me in LA. Sea Org members don't think much about separating spouses, because it happens to them all the time, so that wasn't as much of a concern for Simon.

I said I'd rather wait, but he told me it had to be then or not at all. Despite being tempted with the lure of running my own show in Hollywood and the higher salary he was offering, I told him to find someone else. Not only was I already in the mindset of being off staff and having more freedom, but the idea of working directly with Sea Org people all the time was an additional turn-off.

He said he'd give me some more time to think about it anyway, but then it died down, and that center was never opened. Around that same time Narconon International and Narconon West US were trying to get a new center open in Leona Valley. It was a church-owned property in higher elevation that I believe was used as some sort of school at one point. However, when neighbors and anti-Scientologist activists found out about it they quickly jumped on it and shared information about Narconon and the church, and they never received the zoning permit to allow a rehab program.

8 FINISHING STAFF

After living in Oklahoma for more than five years in tiny spaces, we finally decided to buy a house. We found one that was basically new in a very small development of only a few homes with a view of the lake in the distance. It was only one exit away from Arrowhead and was affordable. We got approved and moved in the first week of February in 2006, just a few days before I stopped working directly for Narconon.

Since Narconon drug education had taken such a beating at the end of 2004 and in 2005 in California and elsewhere, Narconon International and ABLE decided to move forward with plans of a drug prevention outcome study. They sent Bobby Wiggins and JT Daily to join Bobby Newman in Hawaii and got a few private schools to agree to take part in the study. At the same time there were schools in Oklahoma who had also agreed to participate.

The study was commissioned using Marie Cecchini, who had gone to work for the Foundation for Advancements in Science and Education (FASE), which was a Scientologist-run organization that Narconon used to try and validate itself. They had also hired researcher Richard Lennox in an attempt to lend at least some credibility to the study. I wound up assisting with some data collection from a few schools in Oklahoma for the study.

I had lined up a job to work with Eric Mitchell at a company he set up with Kurt Feshbach called Addiction Help Services, which did interventions and referrals. Eric had worked at Chilocco and

Arrowhead and wound up being married to Kurt's oldest daughter Kuryn for a while. I was also starting to build my own first FSM referral website and was occasionally answering some calls for Kent McGregor.

I was suddenly making more than double what I was earning before, but working less than half as much time, which meant I had time to enjoy the new house and work on my film project. I basically did three interventions a month at first, and would take phone calls a couple days per week. Interventions can be very difficult and I don't envy those who do them full-time because they can be such a drain mentally and physically. I eventually quit doing them because a guy came after me with a knife and later rushed at me and had to be restrained by his father and uncle. Some people like the excitement of doing interventions, but I had had enough pretty quickly after that.

For the film, I had flown to LA to meet with Eric Sherman about my script. He walked me through a script revision, business plan and production board complete with shooting schedule and budget. Man, I was excited and life seemed great. I was also playing golf at least two days a week with Kent.

In May I was asked to go to the UK. Narconon Hastings in England (which has since closed) was struggling and Narconon International was tired of sending staff over there to help as well as loads of cash to keep the doors open, so they were asking successful FSMs to help generate some income. The exchange rate made it potentially promising, and I went under the assumption that I would get all of the calls from people looking for help because they didn't have anyone who could do it. Two people had already gone over there before me, David Holtz and Eric Mitchell.

Narconon International wanted Eric to go back over, so instead he and Kurt called me and put the pressure on me to go for two weeks. I really didn't want to go, but was guilted into it. Even though Narconon had some kind of operations in the UK for decades, the facility in Hastings was an old Tudor mansion located by Bobby Wiggins and Jeannie Trahant and a big stink was made about it complete with a grand opening ceremony in March of 2005.

I arrived and was picked up by Alison Withey, who had been involved with Narconon in the UK for many years, and was the Executive Director at one time. I was told that she was removed from her post because she had started a relationship with a recent graduate. I wasn't surprised, because it was such a common theme in every Narconon center I had been to - staff having relationships with recent program graduates.

We went straight to the center and began working, but I immediately noticed that it was not at all like what I was told. Not only was Alison working the phone lines, but also another local FSM named Rob. To make matters more difficult, there were very few people contacting for help and their socialized healthcare meant they could just a get a prescription from their local doctor for free. Most of the reaches were for people addicted to alcohol or opiates, so a prescription seemed fine to most of them. They weren't used to paying for private healthcare services.

I was guilted into going over there for no good reason other than they just wanted my help, but weren't honest about it. I immediately emailed Eric and Kurt and told them the situation and that I wanted to come back right away, but they wanted me to stay and get someone in so that they could get paid for sending me, so I agreed to give it a few days.

After a week I demanded to get back to the U.S. It was pointless for me to be there, I was lonely, I didn't ever adjust to the six-hour time difference and the food and coffee were horribly bland. I finally got my ticket and arranged for Rob to drop me off at a hotel by the Gatwick airport. On the way he took me to see St. Hill, which is were Hubbard lived for many years, where there is a big church, and where the IAS events are held each year. I quickly toured the castle-style church and then off we went. I was expecting for it to be more dramatic for me, but it was actually pretty empty and boring and very anticlimactic. When I finally boarded that plane back to the U.S. the next morning, it was like I was on a lifeboat rescuing me from being lost at sea. Even though it was only a week, it was one of the loneliest weeks of my life.

During this time Erica had changed her job at Arrowhead to one that was more difficult for her because she wasn't trained for it and because of the amount of awful things that had to be dealt with. She was over the hiring and firing of personnel as well as the staff and student ethics sections, meaning she got all of the bad news of people screwing up for a while. She needed a break and wanted to go get some auditing. Since I was earning more, I wrote an email to Gary Smith, warning him that she was about to crash and that if he would give her the time off, I would pay for her to go for a bit and get some relief. He ignored me and instead wanted to keep her on her post since she was doing such a good job.

A few days later she got sick and had enough. It was too much negativity. Gary finally agreed to send her to Los Angeles, but out of punishment instead of reward, unbeknownst to her. He said Arrowhead would pay for her to go to ASHO, but only if she signed another contract extension to show her intent to stay there, so she did.

We arranged for a fellow staff member to stay at our house and take care of our dog, and I decided to drive her out there. We hopped in the car and took off early in the morning in the beginning of July. We drove all day, stopped at a hotel for the night in Arizona, and then drove the rest of the way in the next day. I had arranged time to meet with Eric Sherman again while I was out there to continue working on my film stuff. Rena found out that we were in town, and wanted us to meet in her office on the 4th of July.

She greeted us heartily and was sort of shocked to see me in flip-flops and shorts with an unshaven face, since the years leading up to that she had really only seen me in suits and dress shirts and ties. After some general catching up, she asked what I was doing. She knew that I was working with Eric and Kurt and she also knew about the stuff with Eric Sherman. I told her more of my plan, but then she flat out said that she not only wanted me back on staff, but that she wanted me to be the President of Arrowhead again. She was very sincere and said, "Look, I'm not going to beg you, but I'm telling you that there is nobody else who fits that post and never will. The best thing you can do to help is to be on staff. There isn't a higher purpose."

I thanked her for the compliment, but respectfully declined. I had no intentions of going back on staff for anything.

She said that Tom Cruise looks up to people in the Sea Org and thinks they're the most important people on the planet. I asked her why he didn't join staff then, but all I got back from her was a blank stare.

She paused for a long time, and then said in her South African accent, "Ok. I got it. I hope you find success in your ventures."

After that we said our goodbyes, and it wound up being the last time I'd see Rena in person.

After staying with Erica for a few more days, I finally drove back to Oklahoma, figuring that she would fly back when she was ready.

One day I was about to tee off on the first hole with Kent when she called me, crying. She had been ambushed by Gary Smith, who wanted her to be given a Sec Check, and so she was pulled off what she was working on to do that. After finishing her confessional she went back on to her Grade II, but then suddenly she was told that Arrowhead wasn't going to be paying for her to go in session anymore, though they would pay for her hotel and food. She was hysterical. I was pissed, because I warned Gary ahead of time and said I would pay for her to go to CC Int, which was cheaper, but he waited until it blew up and then sent her to a more expensive place, cross-ordered her to get the Sec Check, and then left her incomplete on the real reason she went out there. I told her not to worry, that I'd figure something out.

I got off the phone and told Kent what was going on.

"Yeah, Gary can be a real asshole," Kent said. "He'll say one thing but then not have your back later if he comes under heat."

I just laughed, shook my head, and then hit the ball.

After the round I went home and looked online for some credit card offers. I called and opened a new card with about a $6,500 limit or something. Her intensives were going to cost $2,600 each. Over the next several weeks, I wound up paying $23,000 for Erica to finish her Grade II and finally come home. I now had two credit cards maxed out and no savings, but she was actually very happy when she returned.

I was doing pretty well with interventions and referrals still and was happy working on the pre-production of my film, playing golf and handling the domestic duties also.

I wound up being able to make a connection with Jason Dohring through Eric Sherman. I wanted to offer him the lead role in my film if I were able to get it financed. He had just finished up his stint on the show Veronica Mars with Kristen Bell and I thought he had some relevance. I flew out to LA to meet with him, and wound up having coffee with him at the cafe behind CC Int. As with most actors, he was much smaller in person than I expected, and was very cordial. He seemed to be extremely distracted, but accepted the script to look over. I had hoped that if he liked it enough that, pending any rewrites, he'd provide a letter of intent that I could use toward obtaining investors. Even better, his dad was worth a few hundred million and could finance it himself if he really liked it.

Soon after that, Jason had been called for a big audition, and wound up landing the role of Josef Kostan, a vampire on the short-lived CBS television series Moonlight opposite Alex O'Loughlin. CBS had ordered the series based on the pilot, but wanted the supporting roles re-cast and only keeping O'Loughlin as the lead. Once Jason got the part, any further discussion with me quickly came to a halt.

Going to be a Dad

Erica got back from LA in August, and by the beginning of September we found out we were going to be parents. Despite things going very well in our lives at the time, we decided that we didn't want to raise a "Narconon child". We wanted to be closer to family, but also to be closer to a church and warm weather, so Georgia was our choice.

When Erica notified the other executives at Narconon Arrowhead that she was not going to work out a second 5-yr contract, but instead just complete her current one, they retaliated against her in several ways - carrying on a tradition in Scientology to punish women who become pregnant and choose to make motherhood their primary role in life. Scientologists believe that being a staff member is the highest purpose you can have and the greatest good for the planet, and if something cuts against that it is somehow "off-purpose" or "out-ethics". Her being pregnant was considered a problem for Narconon. Other women did have kids and either were placed in lower positions because of it, were looked down upon because they had to leave early for motherhood duties or the kids would frequently be hanging around the campus. None of those situations seemed appealing.

She was removed from her senior executive position and placed in a lower position for the remaining months of her contract back in a different division. Her pay was drastically cut as a result and she was shamed for having done something so natural.

Later that fall we put the house up for sale. I placed a For Sale by Owner sign in the yard. The next day I got a call from a woman who wanted to see it. She came by with her two sisters, and wound up making a cash offer that evening after talking it over.

We took a trip to Georgia to find a home, and began looking roughly in between my parents' house and my brother's. I wound up choosing one that had more room, as our plans were to both have offices and work out of the house so that we could be home with our child. We planned on continuing to be FSMs for Narconon.

We went back to Oklahoma for Erica to finish up her contract. We closed on the sale of our home, and were able to pocket just enough money to cover our moving expenses, the down payment on the new house, Christmas presents and to buy a few pieces of new furniture. We wound up renting the home back from the new owner until the agreed-upon move date, which was in the middle of December.

Erica technically still had two weeks left on her contract, but she had vacation time and personal days that could be used. She submitted a request to leave two weeks early to be able to move and have Christmas with family, etc., but that she would work two more weeks from the new home without pay to sweeten the pot. A few middle-level executives tried to disapprove it, but she was given permission from the senior executives, although they said she had to return back on a particular day to "route out" and officially complete her contract.

This was ridiculous, and more people retaliated against her. The Treasury Supervisor Rebecca Poole (Vicki Smith's daughter) and Finance Director Maureen St. Amand wound up withholding her Christmas bonus. Erica was crushed. She had put in five years of very dedicated time only to get slapped in the face because a couple people wanted to make her wrong for no good reason. I wound up writing an additional report and request that she still get her bonus, which wound up being denied, and I let loose on the phone to one of the executives, screaming how utterly stupid they were and that it was insane management tactics such as those that were the reason why so many good staff members leave there.

We eventually got past all of that. After all, it wasn't much money we were talking about, but the principle of it. These were the kinds of things that continued to stack up though, and increase as time went on.

After the New Year we drove back to Oklahoma for her to sign her routing out papers. It happened to be during one of the worst ice storms in history. We drove all day to Paris, TX and then got a hotel for the night, where the temperature was right at freezing and I wasn't chancing it anymore. The next morning the rain had stopped and we continued our trek up into Oklahoma. As we got closer you could see ice in the trees, which were bending over from the weight. By the time we approached McAlester everything was a solid sheet of ice and the entire town was frozen. Trees and electrical poles were snapped in half, power lines were laying on the ground, and the only gas station that was open had a line stretching a few blocks. Still, we pushed on another 20 miles north to the Arrowhead campus.

Erica went in and got her routing form signed by those that were available and necessary. Students and staff were huddled in the facility, which had back-up power. I stayed in the car, and about a half an hour later she walked out and said she was all finished. We left the campus and exited the state park, pointed south again to hit above-freezing temps and hoping for a safe return home. Here we had just risked a treacherous drive with a wife who was almost six months pregnant and spent nearly three full days on the road all for 30 minutes' worth of signatures, all because they wanted to make her pay for leaving staff.

When we got back home both of us were working full-time with Kent McGregor. He and I actually formed a consulting company as an offshoot of one of his companies. Erica was handling most of the incoming phone calls and referring people to Narconon centers, while I got overflow calls and worked on all of the websites. Kent meanwhile got paid to do interventions and also got half the money from all of the referral fees on top of that, despite the fact that Erica and I were doing more than 80 percent of the work. Kent promised that we could take two months off when the baby came as repayment for all we had been doing for him.

On Saturday, April 28th, 2007, Erica and I ran some errands and she wanted to get a new camera before the baby came. We were in the car talking about how it would be a perfect day if she went into labor, even though it was a week early. We went to lunch and then to Target. While walking around the store she was having contractions more regularly and at closer intervals, but they were not close enough to cause alarm yet.

We got back home that afternoon and she went upstairs to take a nap. When she woke up a couple of hours or so later, her water had already broken and so we took off to the hospital. On the way we called our parents. Her mom couldn't get a flight in from Pittsburgh that night, and my parents were in New Orleans, though they left immediately after I called them and began driving back to Georgia.

We checked into the hospital around 6:30 that evening. Our daughter Ella Nicole Catton was born at 10:35 in one of the easiest deliveries the doctor had ever seen. She was perfect, and I have never felt more proud or humbled to be here on Earth. Somehow she was lucky enough to receive the best features of each of her parents.

Suddenly the universe shifted for me, and I now had the extra sense and responsibility of being a father, which is something that I am extremely thankful for each and every day. This girl brings me more joy, laughter and pride than anything else in the world. We have a very special bond and understanding between each other - one that neither has with anyone else.

Just a few days after coming home from the hospital, it became apparent to me that Kent was not living up to his end of the bargain. I was checking the call logs and saw that he wasn't answering the phone. I knew he was out playing golf instead, because that's what he was doing before. He didn't realize the amount of work we had put into growing and handling the call volume, and our income immediately dropped.

I tried to write up an operating agreement with terms that stated he would work harder, but the more I pushed he finally wrote to me saying that he shouldn't have to change his work habits for me. At that point we split, which was in May. He took his websites back and I took mine back. There I was with a brand new house, a newborn baby, a wife who I promised could focus on being a full-time mother and not have to work and no money left in checking or savings.

I became seriously intent on making it work, and somehow pulled it off. I got a couple partial commissions in to make the mortgage and car payments and worked diligently on improving the few websites I had at the time as well as building quite a few more.

Since we were fairly active in the local church, I decided to join WISE and occasionally attend meetings of the Business Expansion Club. I wound up hiring the Executive Director's husband, who was a chiropractor but worked doing other things. Karen and David Morris had a daughter at the same hospital, delivered by the same doctor, just 11 days before our daughter was born. At the time we seemed almost destined to work together and got along well.

Things were starting to improve and I had to find a balance of work and family life, so even though hiring someone else meant less money, it meant a happier life at the time to spend with my wife and daughter.

However, as the months went on things weren't going well be between Erica and me. She had the task of being a new mother, but missed working. She wanted family to be there for support, but only if it was her family. I told her she could do whatever it is she wanted and that I would support her, and she decided she wanted to do some more auditing and take courses at the church in Atlanta, so I watched our daughter when I wasn't working for her to be able to do that.

Despite her having time to do what she said she wanted to do, a wonderfully happy and healthy baby and the fact that we were making enough money to have a comfortable life, we were still having problems. We even asked Karen Morris to help do something called a Chaplain Cycle with us, which is like a basic marriage counseling or dispute resolution.

Here Come the Basics

Something radical happened in the world of Scientology in the summer of 2007. David Miscavige had been on a multi-year kick to "correct" all of the basic books that were written by L. Ron Hubbard in the 1950's. Every summer there is a series of briefings called the Maiden Voyage event as a celebration of the anniversary of the first voyage out to sea of the Freewinds. During this time an "OT Summit" is held, and many of Scientology's top parishioners from around the world attend. They are called OT Ambassadors and are given additional responsibilities on top of regular church members, such as helping to raise funds, ferret out dissidents and go above and beyond to support whatever plans David Miscavige had for the year. Sort of like lower-level Freedom Medal winners, but all of these people are at the top of the Bridge, either OT VII or OT VIII.

In 2007 the Freewinds was docked for a complete refitting, so the events were held in Clearwater instead, and there was buzz of a big announcement. These events were then rebroadcast via DVDs at churches throughout the world, and everyone was expected to attend.

In Atlanta, a conference center was rented out and people were repeatedly called from all over the region to boost, confirm, and re-confirm attendance. My mom went to the event with us, which turned out to be the release of the new Basics, during an event where David Miscavige nearly broke his arm from patting himself on the back in a completely over-the-top display of graphics and pumping music to throw people into a trance.

Everyone in attendance was expected to spend $3,000 for this set of basic books and lectures, and many were encouraged to buy extra sets on the spot. I didn't have $3,000 to spend at the time, so they "let me" get away with buying just the books for $450.

The next day the non-stop harassment for money started. I got call after call saying that it was a mistake to let me buy just the books, and that it was "Command Intention" for everyone to have the complete set. It was not only expected, but you were repeatedly hounded and made to feel like you were somehow not really a supportive member of the group if you didn't fork over the money.

After about a couple of weeks, I finally broke down and purchased the rest of the package, which took two different credit cards and a debit card in order to make up the full amount. I was hoping that the calls would stop once I made the purchase. Those insane phone calls were just the beginning though, as for the next several months Sea Org members from different churches all over the country would call me and ask for more money to donate sets of Basics to new groups and people who couldn't afford them, such as the Narconon centers where staff couldn't purchase them, etc. I was really getting pissed off.

One day I spoke to Bobby Newman, who was still in Hawaii and had become the Executive Director of the fledgling organization. He told me that there were only four people there, but they now had a storage room full of Basics sets and they just kept on showing up. During one of the calls the next day from people asking for money, one woman told me that Narconon Hawaii needed a set, and I laughed. I told her that I didn't know where she got that information from, but that I had just spoken to the guy in charge there and he was asking me if I needed a set because he had about a dozen extra sets that people kept donating. I told her that someone was lying to her, and that I didn't appreciate the constant demands for money and to just send all of the extra sets to other places that needed them, as I was sure that was happening elsewhere in the country.

"So you're not going to give at least a little bit?" she asked.

"Absolutely not." I said.

The calls still didn't stop though. They kept coming over

months and months. People were encouraged to buy 16 sets at a discounted rate of about $29,000 to then resell all 16 of them and make a personal profit of $19,000, as if anyone in the church hadn't already been called and anyone outside the church would even consider buying them. I am aware of at least a couple people who fell for that, though, and the books and CDs simply took up space in their garages because of course nobody would buy them. If I knew of a couple, then there were probably others.

Soon after sales slowed, the church began their library campaign for the Basics. They wanted people to donate $450 per library to get the books shipped to tens of thousands of libraries across the world. This generated many, many millions of dollars in profit for the church, and it was for profit, otherwise if it was merely to make the materials available, they would have had them donated at the cost of printing, especially since they did their own printing so it was even cheaper than ordering them through someone else. Make no mistake; it was only about the money.

I later found out that Yvonne Rodgers from Narconon East US was ordered to clear out much of the organization's savings and spend tens of thousands of dollars on buying sets of Basics, and many other Narconon centers were pinched as well. The more financially robust centers, such as those in Oklahoma and California, were continually hit up to buy even more.

That same library donation money-making scam continued to carry over in subsequent years for other new and re-released books and videos. It still goes on to this day. The latest one I saw was "The L. Ron Hubbard Series", at a cost of $700 each. There have been many, many reports of most of these books being rejected by the libraries and put out on clearance racks for sale for pennies on the dollar, given away and even tossed in the trash. What an incredible waste of time, money, effort and paper - just so the church can make millions more.

Introduction to Flag

Right after the New Year, a team from Flag came to visit the

Atlanta Org. They do some thing each year called the Flag World Tour, where representatives go from church to church and recruit people to come to Clearwater for "Flag-Only Rundowns" and other services there. They had just purchased and renovated the Oak Cove hotel in preparation for the coming renovation of the Fort Harrison.

I had been putting some money on account down there to do a special auditing procedure called L11, as it was touted as being able to "power through the ridges and barriers that hold you back from exceeding in life" or some such nonsense. The problem is that I wasn't approved to be at Flag yet, for the same reason I was routed out of CC Int four years earlier – the depression-fueled suicidal thoughts from 1999.

Erica expressed wanted to go to Flag and do some services there, and we thought she could use the money I had put on account there and maybe another few thousand or so. I already had enough for what she wanted to do, but they wanted more money, of course, for her to be able to be down there and to take advantage of the special introductory prices they were offering. They hyped it up and got her to commit to going the next week.

At that time Ella was only about 10 months old, so we all drove down together. We had to stay at a nearby hotel since I wasn't approved yet. It was only supposed to be a week from start to finish, but after three days Erica hadn't even gone through the full approval process herself. Finally she was ready to start, and we had to visit our registrar, Dave Foster. Dave said he was put on post personally by Hubbard in 1975 and was charged with the responsibility of leading the income for Flag. He of course wanted even more money than what we had already paid, and I was put on the spot right there with the first "You want your wife to have wins and gains, right?" How could I say no, especially with her sitting right there?

There was a problem though, as I didn't have enough room on credit cards at the time to be able to pay for everything. He put me on the phone with a Flag staff member who was in LA at the time named Jeff Mintz. Jeff specialized in helping people to get credit cards and raise their credit limits. He asked me how much I made at that time and what my credit score was, then he said Bank of America had a good 0% interest introductory offer that he thought he could help me get instant approval for. He put me on hold and then did a 3-way call to Bank of America card services, and within minutes I had a new card with a $17,000 limit. He then hung up and called another number and told me what to say in order to get my credit card number and have it be immediately activated without having the physical card.

By the time the whole thing was said and done they knew in less than 30 minutes that I had thousands of dollars more to give them, and they ran the extra few thousand on the brand new card. A moment later, Dave Foster started in on the library campaign for the Basics and asks for a few thousand more. I got upset, but wound up giving another $450 on the spot, which was enough for one library.

As soon as we walked out of there, Erica asked me, "Are you sure you're okay with all of this?" She knew I was put on the spot and instantly incurred several thousand dollars in extra debt.

I just laughed and said, "Well, it's a bit late for that!"

She had her first session right away that night, and was very excited when I picked her up later to have finally started. She thought it was awesome.

By the end of that first week, I really needed to get back to work. I couldn't keep staying in a hotel at $160 per night and watching Ella all day and night while Erica went in session. Somebody had to pay for it all, and it didn't look like she would be finishing any time soon.

We wound up arranging for her mother to fly down from Pennsylvania to watch Ella, and they all checked into the Oak Cove. All in all it took two more weeks, at another $140 per night plus food expenses, etc. What was supposed to only cost a couple thousand quickly became roughly $12,000 for the whole trip. That was my first Flag experience.

When Erica and Ella finally flew back to Georgia, she told me that she wanted to move to Clearwater and that it was the most amazing place in the world. She said she wanted to go back on staff at a Narconon, and that Kurt Feshbach was going to open a Narconon and she wanted to work with Eric and Kuryn.

I told her that we would see how it could work out and to find out how soon the new center would be opening and that we could plan for it then, but she said she wanted to go right away. She even said that she wasn't going to make it if she didn't go, that she hated living in Georgia and that she was going to go there whether I wanted to or not.

More Activity in Georgia

In early 2008 David Morris and I were the top people referring clients to Narconon of Georgia, something that I am ashamed of saying today. Most FSMs wouldn't send people to Mary's facility because of the high percentage of students leaving the program early and having problems, as well as the amount of staff turnover and strife was well known. It was also well known that her disorganization spilled over into the finance area and it would sometimes take months to get paid a commission, whereas it was supposed to be paid within a week. When commissions were paid, they were rarely for the full amounts.

Nevertheless, I felt a connection to Mary since she knew my parents, had been my auditor and performed my wedding ceremony. David also felt a sense of allegiance since he had known Mary for years and was sometimes even paid to go give chiropractic adjustments to staff and students there.

Mary was well aware of my previous accomplishments at Arrowhead, and she asked me to volunteer to come down to help speak to Georgia legislators at their annual display at the Capitol. I did miss that part of my job before, so I agreed to go.

Not only did I help talk to people who came by their display, but I also went around to speak to some of the state Senators and Representatives. In one office, the Senator was very thankful that we were there, as she was the co-author of a bill that tightened restrictions on the sale of methamphetamine precursor ingredients. I explained that I had come from Oklahoma, which was one of the first states to implement a similar bill, and that there was a marked decline in the number of meth labs found in the years following its implementation. She looked very excited and asked if I would stay until after lunch and speak at the committee hearing to share that information in support of her bill. I reluctantly agreed.

At the hearing, I signed in as a speaker, and Mary Rieser also took it upon herself to sign in, as it was open to the public. I spoke about the situation in Oklahoma, while it seemed that Mary just wanted to be able to get her program mentioned in front of those who were on the committee and in attendance. The bill in its form wound up not getting passed that legislative session, primarily due to questions about the funding to get it started.

Although I was unaware of it at the time, Mary wound up sending out a press release several weeks later about Narconon speaking at the hearing. She used my name several times and attributed false quotes to me as well, none of which was run by me for approval. That press release is still online to this day.

Anonymous Protest in March 2008

Anonymous began its very public display of disapproval against Scientology in January of 2008, following the leak of the Tom Cruise IAS Freedom Medal of Valor video and the subsequent attempt by the church to have it removed from the Internet. The Scientology.org site went down from a DDoS attack, and a video was issued warning Scientology that the criminal and inhumane treatment of people would no longer be tolerated. I remember getting chills the first time I watched it. I was afraid of this unknown group, especially since in Scientology you are repeatedly told that anyone who seeks to stop Scientology is inherently evil.

Then word got out that there was going to be live protests at Scientology churches across the world. People in Georgia were summoned to the Org that day to try and outnumber the entheta (bad) with theta (good). I remember sitting inside the rented space and watching as the long line of protesters began walking up the sidewalk across the street. I couldn't believe how many there were, and they easily outnumbered all we could muster by at least three to one. Then the Dekalb County police showed up in full riot gear, and suddenly I got even more worried, unsure of what would happen. Little did I know at the time that the people across the street were much more friendly and caring than the ones who were controlling the church.

We wound up leaving before the crowd dissipated, and as we drove out we saw more protesters with masks holding signs, but by then it was much less scary as it was evident they were peacefully protesting. Later that day David Morris called me. He was down in Clearwater trying to get something handled at Flag, but he wasn't allowed on service there because his ex-wife left Scientology. He told me that there were a couple hundred protesters down at Flag as well and that the Sea Org staff forced everyone to remain inside or only use back and side exits to avoid the protesters. I also wound up viewing video on YouTube as well as news clips from various protests around the world. Apparently more than ten thousand people showed up at live demonstrations in front of Churches of Scientology on several continents. I remember thinking that they didn't know what they were even protesting against, but boy did I have it backwards - I didn't even know what I was really a part of.

9 MOVING TO CLEARWATER

On April 17th we packed up our SUV with our daughter and our dog, complete with suitcases strapped to the luggage rack up top, and left our still-new house full of furniture to start a new chapter of our lives in Clearwater. Despite it being completely against all that we had spent the last year and a half working toward, I felt I was doing what was necessary to try and support my wife.

We signed a six-month lease for a furnished townhouse that was owned by Scientologists through a realtor who was a Scientologist. It was in downtown Clearwater next to the Mace-Kingsley center and Clearwater Academy (both Scientology-related) and within walking distance to Flag. It was also around the corner from the Walgreen's drugstore where Sea Org members would buy toiletries and other stuff on Sunday mornings.

I had just sold two of my websites to other FSMs and made enough for me to buy a couple of intensives at the Tampa Org for myself, for Erica to have a couple at Flag and to pay our bills for a month. Around that time was the first time I started to notice that Erica was getting worse by going to Flag, not better, but I wrote it off as maybe just not being finished with what she was on.

I wound up planning a volunteer trip to D.C. again on behalf of Narconon International. They were trying to start up an alumni association of some type to see what kind of resources and support was available amongst all their graduates, but without a real long-term tracking system or measurement of success, they had no way of really knowing. They printed up a new success brochure and I volunteered my time to go to D.C. and pass them out to all of the Congressmen and Senators who had Narconon centers or offices in their districts.

I had planned out all of their office locations and made a list and just went up without any meetings scheduled. I did call most of their offices ahead of time to be sure they were going to be there rather than back at their district offices. Phil Hart called me on my first day in D.C. to see how it was going so far. I told him I was just pulling up to the Hart Senate Building and he told me that it was actually named after one of his family members – his uncle, I believe - Philip A. Hart. That particular trip didn't turn out to be anything spectacular, mostly small talk with staffers at. I went back to Clearwater the next night after a relatively unfruitful trip.

We had continued offering a fair amount of support to Narconon of Georgia, especially with David Morris living there still. In fact, whenever he was handling the phone calls most of his referrals would go to Narconon of Georgia. One day I called Tracey Stepler, who was working as both a registrar and the case supervisor there. Tracey's husband was the Deputy Executive Director at the Atlanta Org. I was checking in to see if there were any expected arrivals with her that week. She sounded upset and I asked her what's wrong. She told me that Patrick died, but that she really couldn't talk about it. I later found out through a search that she was talking about Patrick Desmond, a student of theirs.

Despite the feeling of obligation to help them, that made me sick to hear. I had already been frustrated by the number of people who didn't complete the program, the disorganization from Mary Rieser and her inability to pay commissions on time, and that sealed it for me as far as concentrating on helping their specific facility. I was still a True Believer back then, but I sold the main website of mine that was a feeder for Narconon of Georgia to another Atlanta-area Scientologist, who happened to be Tracey's ex-brother-in-law. Down the road Patrick's family wound up filing a lawsuit against Narconon for negligence and wrongful death.

The extra money from the sale of the Georgia site offered a

bit of help and I put half into savings and half towards credit card debt.

Meanwhile I was getting auditing at the Tampa Org and had started New Era Dianetics (NED). Once again I found myself believing that I had been a part of Scientology the previous lifetime and that I had already reached the state of Clear and above.

The Senior Case Supervisor came in one day and told me that the e-meter only reacts to what I think and feel and can validate anything that I resolve in my own mind. She said that just because the e-meter indicated something doesn't make it true. She was a highly trained auditor at a Class VIII and had also completed OT VIII. At first this upset me quite a bit. However, much later I realized that she was actually right. In an auditing session the person is encouraged to believe that just because the e-meter reacts a certain way or seems to validate a thought or memory, it must be true, but that absolutely isn't the case. Despite this, many Scientologists say they "know" something happened because it was validated by the e-meter in session. Nevertheless, at that time I thought it must have been true for me.

I fought with people there to be able to go to Flag, and had a special program put together by Flag. The end of that program resulted in me getting to go do another Clear Certainty Rundown there. I finally got approved to go to Flag and was setting up to do my CCRD. I never felt comfortable there. I would walk around and feel like I didn't belong there. Back then it was a self-deprecation in believing I was somehow unworthy or not accepted. In reality, it was my own natural warning system telling me to get the hell out of there.

In preparation for the CCRD I had seen two different auditors. One of whom had a very eerie, wide-eyed stare who had to do a PTS interview with me about a cold I recently had. He wanted to stress clearly that the definition of a Suppressive Person to them was someone who was opposed to helping others and opposed to Scientology – as if only people who didn't want to help others would be against Scientology.

I finally got to the third auditor who was going to perform the actual CCRD. I did my best to describe what it was but then it came back again that I wasn't Clear. I got upset and said it was bullshit. She then immediately started asking me if Flag missed a withhold on me and wanted to know what overts I had committed against Flag since I was being critical of them. What a mess. It was another sign that it was all bullshit and I should have never gone back. How many more signs did I need? Apparently it wasn't enough.

Moving to Harbor Oaks

In October of 2008 we moved into an historic neighborhood in Clearwater called Harbor Oaks, which is just a few blocks from Flag. It was an old colonial home built in 1937 and had been lived in at one time by Kurt Feshbach and his family. Like many homes in the area, the garage had been converted into a guest house and there was a small pool in the backyard as well. Despite sounding stately, it was actually a pretty modest two-story colonial that was overpriced because of the neighborhood. We signed a lease purchase and were going to rent it for a year, hoping that we could make more money to qualify for a loan within 12 months. We also gave them a non-refundable down payment, basically forwarding the money we got from the people looking to do the same thing with our house in GA.

The little guest house out back was going to be my office, but it was rundown. I painted it and put in a new tile floor to try and fix it up a bit. I didn't like the house overall and it was too expensive, but it was what Erica really wanted and I was trying my best to please her.

At the time my referral websites really started to pick up, and my friend JT Daily and his wife had moved to Clearwater as well. JT and I began working together to build a team. I was sharing with him all the things that were successful for me and he began creating his own websites as well, including investing a lot of money to purchase a premium domain and to pay others to build some sites in addition to what I was doing.

JT's then-wife, Corina, was hired as a nanny for John Travolta and Kelley Preston's daughter. She was often gone on trips around the world with the family. She met some resistance getting approval from Flag though, at first, because when she was a young child in Canada her dad committed suicide after returning from Flag. He was a member of the Canadian rock band Chilliwack and her mother continued to raise her in Scientology even after that. The President's office at Flag screened several employees for John and Kelly.

I honestly feel bad now for kids raised in Scientology because they have a completely different view of the world, all shaped by one man. They are taught at an early age to ignore negative stories about Scientology and to stay away from people who are critical of it. They then become adults with sheltered mental compartments who speak a different language and think they know more about life than others because that is what they are led to believe.

One time when JT was sick he told me that he had been talking to Corina, and Travolta overheard her asking him what he was taking to feel better. He said John got on the phone and began telling him about a special type of enema that helps relieve flu symptoms, including giving details. He said he was grossed out and couldn't believe that John Travolta was providing instructions on how to give himself an enema and that he was embarrassed even listening to it.

JT also had maintained contact with Amy Bloustine, formerly with the DEA museum, who had gone on to work for the Partnership for a Drug-Free America. He was chosen to work on a new online campaign with them where he did some voiceover work and they created a special avatar on part of their website. While only being paid minimally, he wanted to keep the connection for future possibilities. He also didn't want to tell Narconon about it because he knew they would try and get involved and report it up through the church and potentially mess things up, just like they had done with the DEA museum.

All was not bright and shiny though despite having fun working with JT and growing the websites. On New Year's Day we got two calls from people in Oklahoma. Jean Lafitte had committed suicide at his cabin on Narconon Arrowhead's campus.

I couldn't believe it. He was my friend, and I was angry for how he was under appreciated and generally undervalued as a person there. It was surreal.

That wasn't all that was going wrong at Arrowhead. After a dramatic expansion period between 2001 and 2005 during which the income went from $7 million in 2001 up to $13 million in 2005, it then began to taper off. Within the next few years dropped back down to $8 million or below and they were struggling. Their payroll had ballooned since they wound up having more employees than students. The client enrollment had peaked at more than 250 students on the program all the way down to less than 100. It rose back up and leveled off somewhere around 120 to 150.

At the height of things for me in mid 2009 we were getting roughly four or five people each week into a Narconon center or related program, and I was clearing about $4,000 per week. Since I was splitting everything that came in with JT or others who answered the phones, I averaged about $950 each per student arrival because of the different costs per center and because of the number of people who didn't complete the full program so either they didn't pay the full amount or received refunds.

At first glance I was doing great, but at the same time Erica was having problems and going in session at Flag, which was costing me between $3,400 and $6,800 per week. Also, the people who were renting our house wound up moving out so I was responsible for that mortgage again. My day generally included getting my daughter ready for preschool, taking her, working all day, then taking a break around 5 to help get dinner ready and take care of my daughter. Then I would go back to work from about 9 PM until midnight.

Unlike many other FSMs or referral groups, whenever I worked the phone lines I always offered multiple options. I know most Narconon FSMs are very deceptive and lie about multiple things. Many of them first ask if they are looking for a private facility and have the ability to pay. If yes, they continue on and start talking about a "biophysical program", being careful not to mention the word Narconon so they don't type it into a search engine. If they say they don't have money then the FSMs usually dump the call and give them the government hotline, which is 1-800-662-4357.

I would either find multiple listings for them on the phone via the Substance Abuse and Mental Health Services Administration's (SAMHSA) website or I would e-mail them a listing of all the programs in their area that fit the description of what they were looking for. I still did that even for those I was referring, as I believed it was important for them to compare programs for themselves and make the decision. Actually caring for the people on the other end of the phone was a huge part of what made me successful, I believe. However, I was fooling myself in thinking that the registrars at Narconon would actually tell them the truth about what the program is and does, or that the program really even qualified as a treatment center. If I was ever asked how I got paid, I'd tell people I received commissions for facilities, but that 98% of the people we help we received no money for, which was true.

No matter how successful I thought I was, I was falling further and further into debt and my health was starting to fade from all the pressure, lack of sleep and tremendous stress. Every time Erica's hours at Flag were about out, I'd get another call from Dave Foster looking for more money. I'd often have to piece together the funds on several different credit cards, including having to juggle when the statement deadlines were to know how much I could put on which card on which day and what the minimum payments would be. I eventually drained what little savings we had accumulated, which was supposed to be for the down payment on our house.

We also had people from the IAS show up unannounced routinely. One Saturday afternoon we were hanging out by the pool and two people came walking around the back of our house. Ultimately they wanted me to increase my status level. I had given close to $25,000 to the IAS in all of our names combined up to that point, and they wanted me to become a Patron, which was a $50,000 level. They had a "fabulous deal" that would give me 20 percent off and I could "save" several thousand by giving them another $22,000 or so.

It was a difficult time, and Erica and I still weren't doing well.

I was getting frustrated at the amount of money it was costing as well as the lack of results that were being produced at Flag. From what I saw, she was getting worse and not better. I kept getting all these explanations of different reasons and parts of NED that she was on, saying that hopefully the next auditing procedure would be the one to finally handle what was going on with her.

I got mad one day and asked her if they could put her on the "knock it the fuck off" rundown. I thought it was hilarious of course, but she felt incredibly invalidated and relayed that to her auditor. I later found out that her auditor and other people at Flag indicated that I may be part of her problem if I had any "CI" (counter-intention) to her Bridge Progress. She would blame me for it taking so long, her doing poorly and it costing so much, saying it was actually my fault.

Here I thought that I was doing all I could to help her, but was just getting frustrated with it, yet the church was playing me against her and driving a wedge further between us while they had her in their clutches.

Finally Erica attested to the state of Clear at Flag. I was completely wiped out in every way after spending more than $60,000 just in a three-month span for her. It would have been much more, but she had rejoined staff at Narconon East US by then and started to receive half-price discounts again for the last few intensives. I spent $90,000 on Scientology in 2009.

I then felt like I needed some relief. Erica knew that I was completely burned out and she met with Dave Foster. They decided they wanted to help me, but of course the help they were offering was going to cost me a ton of money and I had none. I called my dad and borrowed a few thousand dollars to buy one intensive for myself so I could do some repair auditing. Even though I was fed up with Flag, I was still under the mindset at the time that Scientology was the only thing that could ultimately fix things. I did go in session and felt a bit better at first, but then just got more frustrated as I was told I needed to buy another package of intensives and to just keep moving on the Bridge, but that wasn't working and I stopped going in and didn't buy more intensives for myself. I just went back to work, paid back my dad and focused on trying to pay off the credit cards while also trying to replenish some savings.

One night a knock at my door at 9:30 revealed a man I had never met, escorted by a female Sea Org member. His name was Howard Becker, and he invited himself in and said it was urgent. He told me that COB (Miscavige) had ordered that Flag raise $10 million and the deadline was approaching. He said they were very close to their target and needed me to give at least a couple thousand, but I couldn't do it. I told him I really didn't have the money.

Howard didn't take no. Here was a man that I had never met before sitting in my dining room demanding money from me because David Miscavige demanded money. "It's Command Intention," he said. There was that phrase again. He went on to tell me that the money was needed for a big online and television advertising campaign that they had already committed to, so they had to have the money. Once again, I gave in to the pressure and gave $500.

Turns out that Howard was an infamous "field disseminator" for the IAS who went around collecting donations and getting paid 10% for the money he raised as his full-time job, not unlike what Bobby Wiggins used to do on the weekends years earlier.

The Freedom Magazine Article

One day we were hanging out at home and saw that we had a new copy of Scientology's *Freedom* magazine. In it was a bizarre article about former church executives, talking about abuse and violence and even admitting that it happened. The article didn't use their real names, but called them things like "Kingpin" and "The Adulteress".

It didn't make much sense, and actually made me much more curious as to what was going on. JT read it and said he wouldn't be surprised if people were knocked around a bit, but that he didn't think much of it. Neither of us realized at the time that it was in response to the now-legendary Truth Rundown series in the *St. Petersburg Times*. We hadn't read it and all Scientologists are encouraged to not read or watch negative stories about Hubbard or anything Scientology-related in newspapers, magazines, on television or online.

Working with Narconon Louisiana

By late summer 2009, JT wasn't working with me as much because he had gone off to Texas for some auditing and I had to find a replacement for him handling my phones, so I did. The other guy liked working with the Narconon in Louisiana, and we eventually set up an agreement with them where they paid me for the leads and the other guy tried to send as many to them as possible.

In September of that year, actress Mackenzie Phillips was about to make national headlines with her book, which mentioned that she had gone to Narconon Louisiana for her addiction. I wrote a press release for them and helped them send it out. Celebrity Centre International got angry and told Clark to order no further promotion, because Mackenzie's big revelation in the book was that she had an incestuous relationship with her father and they didn't want Narconon or Scientology to be connected to that "entheta". Once again, CC Int was dictating actions for Narconon.

Meanwhile, I was taking the opportunity to start writing a book of my own. It was my first attempt at diverging from Narconon by looking at other alternative forms of treatment, though I didn't exactly stray too far. I started writing it in late 2009 and decided to call it *The New Face of Recovery*. While it may have had some good intentions to branch out and some good ideas on public policy, it still of course had to promote Narconon and Scientology, whether directly or indirectly.

Moved to Freedom Drive

There was a development down there called Clearwater Village that was started by a couple Scientologists. The road is Freedom Drive and has about a couple dozen high-end homes and townhouses on it. Since we couldn't afford to buy the house in Harbor Oaks, we lost our down payment and had to move out at the end of the 12 months. We were able to rent one of the luxury townhouses on Freedom Drive from the Scientologist family who owned it for less than we were paying for the other house. It was basically still brand new and felt way better to me than the 70 year-old house we had just moved from.

During this time I continued working on my writing and websites and took care of most of the stuff at home while Erica worked for Narconon East US. The major financial bleeding had temporarily subsided since neither one of us were actively going in session, and I was focused on trying to pay off the massive credit card debt and rebuild some savings.

Digging Deeper

There was a time toward the end of 2009 when I had seriously considered going back on staff at Narconon, such as working for Narconon International remotely to be a spokesperson again. Before I made any type of decision though, I wanted to speak with Rena Weinberg.

I hadn't seen Rena since July 4th, 2006 and hadn't spoken to her since September of that year. I had asked many times where she was, including asking people at ABLE and Narconon International. Nobody knew for sure, or if anyone did, they wouldn't tell me. The only thing ever said was that she was "uplines" doing something, implying that she was working with management.

I had kept her husband Brian's cell phone number from when

he had called me one time asking for a donation. He was The Way to Happiness Foundation representative for ABLE. When Brian answered he was surprised to hear from me. He was even more surprised when I asked him where his wife was. He told me that he knew, but that he couldn't tell me and that it put him in sort of a weird situation. I asked if he could get a message to her and he said he would try. I simply asked him to have her contact me if she could because she needed to know what was going on in the Narconon network and I needed her advice.

After I hung up I was left with even more of a mystery. Where was she, and why couldn't he tell me? What was she really doing and why would the church damage ABLE by removing their President, Executive Director and Narconon representative? What was really going on?

Forced to redo the Purif

Since I was becoming more and more fed up and defiant against the church, they used a reference about having an "unflat Purif" against me, stating that I must not have gotten the full benefit and that I had to redo it. I argued and argued but got nowhere. I was told that I could not do anything further until I went through the sauna program again.

Multiple people plead their cases to me to just comply, and that they were the experts and I shouldn't try to second-guess them. I eventually was beat down enough that I complied, as I was at a complete standstill. The saunas at Flag are in the Ft. Harrison Hotel, which had been newly renovated. It has a nice gym, locker rooms, courtyard, pool, hot tub and Koi pond, so at first glance it would be a very nice place to just hang out, but I wasn't there to hang.

I started going in early October and was doing it very thoroughly, running, sweating, drinking plenty of water, eating vegetables, taking all of my vitamins and Niacin - all of it perfectly. I kept moving up in Niacin levels but nothing was happening other than a short, red flush every couple of days or so. I kept saying that I was done and that nothing was going to happen because I didn't need to do it again, but all I got back was to keep going.

One day a woman from New Jersey asked me if I had seen ABC's *Nightline* the night before, which I hadn't. So when I got home I looked it up online and watched the episode on their website, which was when Martin Bashir was interviewing celebrities and then Tommy Davis. Bashir asked about the Xenu story and Tommy stopped him and said he found that offensive and that if he asked about that again he'd walk out of the interview. A few seconds later Bashir rephrased the question and Tommy ripped off his microphone and walked off screen. He looked like a childish fool.

What wasn't as widely known was that Davis had been grilled by NBC affiliate KESQ reporter Nathan Baca that aired in March of 2009, which I hadn't seen by then either. Baca asked about the Xenu story and Davis admitted he knew what he was referring to and that it was "church scripture" and that he found it offensive. There was also the interview in 2008 on CNN where Davis claimed he didn't know about the Xenu story. So by October of 2009 when Bashir's piece ran, Davis had been thoroughly reprimanded about his on-air handling of that question and so he handled it by simply walking off.

It struck me as extremely unbecoming, as here was the spokesperson of my church - someone who by default was an extension of my practices - acting like a spoiled brat and making Scientology look even worse than it already did.

After I watched that interview I saw a recommended video about Jenna Miscavige Hill, who is David Miscavige's niece. She had left the church and did an interview with *Nightline* the year prior. I had no idea. I was shocked about her interview and how she spoke of her mistreatment growing up in the church, including being cut off from her own parents and being forced to do manual labor at a young age. The story also included a bit about Astra Woodcraft, who had joined the Sea Org at 14 and was married inside it at 15. She too was cut off from members of her family.

Now my interest was piqued. I started to dig a bit deeper and wound up reading the full Truth Rundown series of articles from the *St. Petersburg Time*. It was then that I found out about Marty Rathbun and Mike Rinder, and I was even more surprised.

After watching and reading these interviews, I was certain that there was more going on that the church was trying to hide. I could tell things were messed up. After a couple more days in the Purif, I finally walked in one day and said I wasn't going in until I had an interview with someone because I was done.

I went and saw someone in the Qualifications Division - Tracy Lemos. I had seen her before about other upsets regarding my Clear Certainty Rundown and how that was messed up, and now I was back with this. She tried to convince me that I just needed to go back and listen to the case supervisor because they knew what was best for me, but I continued to argue with her. She finally gave up and sent me to ethics.

When I saw the MAA in the ethics department, Daniel, he did a metered interview with me. He asked if I had done anything I shouldn't have. I told him about watching and reading the negative stories about the church online. He then tried to tell me how I couldn't progress in Scientology if I look at that stuff, warned me not to look at any of it again, and I had to sign a promissory note stating that I wouldn't.

Daniel also pulled out a report that a Scientologist wrote on me regarding my book. It stated that I talked about the sauna program without giving credit to L. Ron Hubbard or Narconon. That was a lie, though. I was never shown the report or who wrote it. I told Daniel I would give him a copy of the book to see for himself.

After all of that, I still refused to go back to the Purif, and so I just ended off at a standstill again.

I sort of chilled out for a few months, though Erica and I continued to have problems. We frequently had people from the Chaplain's office at our house to talk to us and try to help sort things out, though there were only temporary "cease fires."

More Fundraising

The fundraising instances continued incessantly. One day I was walking down a hallway in the Oak Cove at Flag when Sonya Jacques stopped me. She was the top registrar and wife of the Captain of Flag. She was the reg for my mom and said, "Luke, I need your mom to go ahead and buy her next package of intensives. I need your help. Your dad has the money in his SEP account (Self-Employed Retirement Plan). Will you reg him to do it?"

"Um, I don't think so," I said. "Frankly, I'm having issues with regging as well and I don't think it's a good idea for me to call them about giving you more money."

"Ah, I see," see replied judgmentally, "You have mutual out-ruds," which meant that I had some non-survival agreement that they shouldn't give the money to the church.

Another night I had three Sea Org staff show up at my house to "chat" for a while, which wound up with them in my home office trying to convince me to cough up at least $2,000 toward an e-meter, if not by the whole thing outright for $3,600.

Then there was the night that Sascha Berlin from the Chaplain's office and another guy came over to hang out. We talked quite a bit, but my mom was in town so no regging occurred inside. After more than an hour I walked them outside to grab a smoke with them before they left. After lighting a cigarette I was hit with, "So, you know we can't go back to our senior with no money after being gone for a couple hours, right?"

Just when I thought they were there to actually be social after work (silly me, Sea Org members aren't really allowed to have friends on the outside), I was told, "We'd like you to do at least two G's."

Really? Were they pretending to be friendly just for the money, or did they actually want to be friendly but would be punished if they didn't bring back money to the coven? By actual inspection, I believe it was the latter. I didn't give them two thousand dollars that night, but I did give them another $500.

This was how it went, literally the entire time living in Clearwater. People were frequently calling you and showing up at your house and hitting you up in the hallway or outside a building or after course, etc. - always asking for money.

I had someone follow me out to my car, a young guy named Tegan in the Sea Org who had already been divorced once and liked to come over to our house. He frequently hit on Erica and this time was going after me for more money. He climbed in and pretended to be friendly for a bit, then pulled out a donation slip and said, "I can't just hang out. I have to come back with money." So I gave him $100.

There were young kids involved, too. There is something called the Cadet Org, for children 12 and older (usually) whose parents were in the Sea Org. I distinctly remember a very young-looking Asian girl who could hardly speak English hanging out at the HGC waiting room at Flag. She would walk around with a pitiful look on her face and just hold out donation forms. These vultures were depriving a little girl of a normal life and having her panhandle for donations for a very wealthy organization. It was disgusting, and I regret not saying anything about how hundreds of adults walked past her every day and not one stood up for her right to actually be a child and have a normal life. It hurts to think of what it must be like for a kid growing up in that environment. All they know is that they work and do what they're told.

Every department at Flag was given a weekly quota for fundraising and/or book sales. If they didn't meet those quotas they would have to spend time in the call center late at night after their regular post duties. This was confirmed by multiple Sea Org members. Most of them didn't want to do it, but they were forced to do it.

Each year the L. Ron Hubbard birthday event is held in Clearwater on or around March 13th. I went that year with JT and we wound up sitting next to the new Captain of Flag, Harvey Jacques, who sat silently with a scowl on his face the entire time. I distinctly remember seeing David Miscavige up on stage bragging about the "biggest Objectives boom in Flag's history". It was so significant to me because I knew that almost all of the people who were doing them were ordered to re-do them right after many of them had already been ordered to re-do their Purifs. He was promoting it as some amazing feat, yet it was the same people doing something they had already done. I think people doing stupid shit over again only equals a "boom" in Scientology events.

The Today Show and New York Times

Things just weren't adding up. One day Erica's parents were visiting us, and I walked downstairs to find them both watching the *Today* show, featuring Christie King Collbran. It was a follow-up to her story that appeared in the *New York Times*. She was a young woman who had left the Sea Org after refusing to have an abortion. She was labeled an SP by the church for getting auditing from Marty Rathbun, who had left the church years earlier. She talked about being disconnected from her parents, and the fact that they wouldn't even see their grandson. She also talked about coerced abortions in the Sea Org, and charging former Sea Org members tens of thousands of dollars to pay in order to receive any further services, which is called a freeloader bill.

Erica's parents asked what that was all about and I basically deflected it, as I did know of some people who had left the Sea Org and had had children without being declared an SP, so it must have been more to the story. I was able to shut down the line of questioning, but I think it made me even more curious than them. That night, after having sworn to not look at any more negative stories about the church, I went and read the whole article about Christie, and started looking into other things again.

More Fighting, Chaplain's Office, Marriage Counseling

Erica and I had been fighting, a lot. Most of the time our fights were about money, Narconon and Scientology. They were also about domestic duties though. There was a constant struggle for who got who's way rather than coming to understandings and agreements. Usually she felt she was right because she was on staff with Narconon and compliant with the church. Of course there are two sides though and I know I wasn't pleasant to be around either. I'm not going to claim total innocence.

We had many nights were people from the Chaplain's office would come over after dinner and talk with us for a while. In addition to trying to help us with the marriage they were often there to try and talk me into getting back in the course room or moving on my next Bridge action or something.

We actually became friends with some of these people, such as Sascha, who was a young German guy. There was also a girl named Sara and another named Sondra who came over frequently, and each of them would bring different people sometimes, or come over together. They also all loved seeing Ella and playing with her a bit. It was sort of sad to see, especially looking back on it all, because these young people didn't have a life outside of the Sea Org, worked ridiculously long hours often without a day off and weren't allowed to start a family of their own. I noticed the population of the Sea Org appears to be getting younger. Not only are many of the members second-generation Scientologists, but I believe it also has to do with younger people being more impressionable and take orders or accept conditions easier than someone with more experience in life.

Eventually they gave up on handling us, and said we needed to do Scientology marriage counseling. This is where one auditor asks the husband or the wife on the meter, "What have you done to [the other]?" and "What have you withheld from [the other]?" alternating questions until you have a floating needle, while the spouse sits and watches silently. Then the spouses trade positions.

We finally agreed to do it. I knew I wasn't hiding anything so I would say whatever came up. The problem is that they wanted to charge us $6,800 to do it, when it used to cost $1,200. One girl got approval for us to do it for the original price if we also bought a set of the newly-released Advanced Clinical Course lectures (ACCs) for another $5,000.

We agreed and went in to get started. The first day was pretty awful, but by the third day we felt we were done and had nothing more to say.

We had put an offer on a townhouse on Freedom Drive that was listed as a short sale, and it happened to get accepted, and we thought there was a chance to save the marriage after all.

The Narconon Meeting in Dallas

Then in April we went out to the Narconon International Executive Director's Conference, which was being held in Dallas, TX that year for some reason. We flew out on a Thursday night. Staff members from Narconon centers all over the world were in attendance, including places across Europe, Asia and South America.

Friday during the conference Rubina Qureshi from ABLE spoke. She had been promoted to be a VP and she was going over the new website for the church that showed Narconon as one of its programs. Almost immediately the room got uncomfortable. Someone from Narconon Sweden asked, "Why would the church of Scientology list Narconon on its website when we spend so much time and effort trying to claim we are separate?" It was the million dollar question - why, indeed.

"The church is proud of Narconon," Rubina replied, "and Narconon should be proud of the church."

Then, silence. She had no idea how much Narconon tried to distance itself from Scientology when it came to selling the program, but there it was for everyone in the room to see without question and explained by a Sea Org member at the organization in charge of Narconon, it is a part of Scientology.

Narconon to this day still says William Benitez read *Fundamentals of Thought* by L. Ron Hubbard as inspiration for the program, but the full book title is *Scientology: Fundamentals of Thought*. In addition, Benitez was discarded as any sort of active member of the organization early on, sans some PR appearances, and is still exploited today as the founder of Narconon, yet no recompense is given to his widow or posterity. His image and story are plastered all over Narconon websites to "prove" they're not a part of Scientology, yet they pay no royalties to the estate of the person they claim is the founder of the program. I would think she would have an excellent case in court to receive back payment for 45 years' worth. In order to not owe money, in my opinion, they would have prove that they have been lying this entire time about the program's connections and controlling entities. Maybe June Benitez will step forward one day and share the full story about her husband and what the church did to him.

Later that day we all went over to the new church of Scientology in Dallas to see their new Ideal Org. We had dinner there and got a tour of the place. Like Narconon centers, churches are also supposed to have graduation ceremonies on Friday nights where people get certificates and a chance to speak for completing a course or auditing level. I was expecting there to be more people there, but there were double the number of staff as there were parishioners, and entire course rooms weren't even opened up. In short, the place was empty.

We flew back to Clearwater after the conference on Sunday, and I was hoping that things would smooth out, but my nerves didn't last much longer there. There happened to be an IAS reg named Michelle - the same one who had shown up unannounced on numerous occasions - who called me one day. I had read news stories online about misappropriation of funds and how the Ideal Org campaign was a con game real estate scam. I told her I really wasn't interested in giving the IAS any more money unless I knew exactly where it was going and that I wanted to see a balance sheet of the funds received and how they were spent.

She said they didn't do that but that the evidence of where it's spent is all around, including the Ideal Orgs. She said she spoke to an Executive in Dallas and that they were booming now that they have their new building.

"That's a fucking lie!" I shouted at her through the phone. "I was just there two weeks ago and it was empty, I mean plastic still covering chairs and course rooms unopened. Empty!"

She was shocked and didn't know what to say. She said it must have been a mistake, or maybe I was just there at a bad time, but I explained we were there on a Friday night and there wasn't even a graduation there were so few people there. She said she would look into it and let me know, and that if we could meet in person she'd give me a more detailed briefing on how the money was being spent. I told her I just wasn't interested, and we ended the call. That was the last time I spoke with her. She did try and call a few times over the next several months, but I never answered or returned her calls.

I got another series of calls after the Dianetics Anniversary Event, eleven in all in a two-day period. I kept not answering the phone because I could see that it was a church number from Los Angeles. After ignoring the first ten calls I finally got pissed and answered. It was Kit Whittle, the current Executive Director of ABLE. She was one of several Sea Org members working the call center phone lines in LA because they were given quotas to sell special new copies of *Dianetics* for $500 each. I told her she was crazy and I had no intention of buying a book for that price and that she needed to understand that I lived in Clearwater and got calls and visitors all the time looking for money.

The ACCs that were released earlier were the most expensive set of materials at the time. They were "discounted" to $5,000 as an opening price and later went up to $7,500 and are now back down to $5,250, which is listed as a savings off the full price of 10K. When they came out Scientologists were already completely strapped and many were in major debt and/or some were losing homes and filing for bankruptcy. Very few people could afford them or could even be bullied into buying them like the other large releases such as the Basics ($3,000) and the Congress lectures ($2,000).

JT was on course at the Advance Org at Flag, called the Sandcastle, working on some Basics courses. He had attested to Clear as well and was preparing to do his Solo Auditor Course to start his OT levels. Most of the people in the course room were already on OT levels. He told me one day after course two Sea Org members shut the doors and wouldn't let anyone leave until they either bought the ACCs or at least gave money toward them. He said they were berating the people on course saying it was their duty as Scientologists to buy them and that they owed it to COB for making these available. "COB" stands for Chairman of the Board of Religious Technology Center, a moniker that church members use to refer to David Miscavige.

JT said he was pretty freaked out by that and wound up pleading poor but still gave $100. He said after that he started driving his old car to course instead of his much newer and nicer BMW so that they wouldn't hound him so much for money.

10 LEAVING CLEARWATER, SORT OF

One day Erica was going in session with some leftover hours she had on account still to do something. She came home and told me that she wanted to transfer back to Arrowhead and move to Oklahoma. I was all over it in a second. I was so excited for an opportunity to get the hell out of Clearwater, that I highly encouraged it.

Once she got approval from Phil Hart at Narconon Int and others, I wrote to Phil personally and wanted to make sure that he was going to back her up on this, because I was going to facilitate the whole move and couldn't afford to mess around if it didn't go smoothly. He assured me it would be fine, though Phil had not been the most trustworthy person, in my opinion, given his continued efforts to put aside doing what's right in favor of collecting money. He would often call staff members as well as FSMs and have a Sea Org member on the phone with him, usually someone from ABLE, and they would ask for donations to the church for books or for the IAS. Yes, the Executive Director of Narconon International called staff and FSMs to get money on behalf of the church, while he was at work.

I quickly started looking at homes online, which is one of my favorite pastimes. I've always been a fan of real estate and architecture and actually love the home-buying process, so it was exciting to start looking for something again in Oklahoma. The good and bad part about it though was that there wasn't much inventory for the size, location and style of home we wanted. However, I got it narrowed down to a dozen homes, including one in our old neighborhood, and arranged to have a realtor set up some showings for me. I booked a flight and headed out in mid-May.

By the end of the day I had pretty much made a decision. I found what could be turned into a perfect home. There were others that I liked the actual house better, but not the lot, or the neighborhood but not the home, but one had the best combination. When I showed them all to Erica and told her which one I thought, she said she'd trust me and I picked one. I emailed the realtor the next day and put in an offer. Soon we were under contract and had set a closing date for the middle of July.

Before we were going to move, though, Erica was told she also had to redo her Purif. Although she wasn't happy about it, after pushing me so hard to redo mine, she wanted to go ahead and get hers done, so she started. After a couple of weeks she was begging me to come back in. Despite some initial resistance, I agreed to go back in for her. At that time Kirstie Alley was also redoing her Purif, and John Travolta and Kelly Preston's daughter was in there as well with a friend, even though they were only around twelve years old.

I was back in the Purif for just three days when I got a raging migraine. It was so bad I threw up and couldn't even think straight. Of course we weren't allowed to take any type of over-the-counter pain relievers though. It took me several hours to fall asleep that night from the headache. I swore that I was done with the Purif for good and didn't want to go back to Flag for any services at all.

Erica, however, kept on going. She was having lots of stuff happen. Soon we had our closing scheduled and went and officially bought our new house. I was just focused on moving. We had set a date for the first week of August. As moving time got closer, I drove out to Oklahoma to buy a washer and dryer, get the satellite TV and internet hooked up, and to paint a couple of the bedrooms. Once I finished I left my car at the house and flew back to Florida to finish packing.

We wound up pushing the movers back another week because

Erica hadn't finished her sauna program yet. As the days kept going she asked me to postpone it again, but I refused. I told her that I had already rescheduled it once and if she's not done then she can just fly out afterward. She wasn't happy about it at all and said I wasn't being supportive, yet I was the one handling the whole move. I do have to admit though that I was anxious to get the hell out of there, so that was my primary motivation at the time.

Moving day soon arrived and Ella and I dropped off Erica at the Fort Harrison so she could do the Purif and check into the hotel until she finished. The movers started to do their thing and Ella and I finally took off about three in the afternoon with our dog, Oliver. We were both exhausted, and I was looking at an 18-hour drive ahead of us. I drove until about 2 AM and finally had to pull over and try to sleep. I didn't want to get a hotel. I just wanted to get there.

After only getting a couple hours of sleep I decided to push on the rest of the way. The sun came up as we were driving through northeastern Texas. I stopped for another cup of coffee and some juice for Ella in Paris and then made our final push home. We pulled into our new driveway at 10 AM. I was so tired that I went inside and lay down on the air mattress I had left there from before. Ella and Oliver went to sleep as well and we crashed for almost three hours.

After I got up and took a shower, we went to the store to get some food for the house, and right after that the moving truck showed up. It was 104 degrees that day, but it all got unloaded and into the house. Over the next couple of days Ella and I tried to get things unpacked and set up – at least the most important things.

Erica was still going for a while back in Clearwater, and I felt like I needed some help so my mom came out for a few days. One of those days it finally rained and cooled things off a bit. I have a great picture that my mom took of Ella dancing in the rain. We loved that house and all the outdoor space. Nearly three weeks after we arrived in Oklahoma, Erica was able to hop on a plane and join us at the end of August. She started working back at Narconon Arrowhead at the beginning of September.

I kept Ella home with me all day for two more months, and we had tried to hire a nanny to come to the house so I could work. That plan didn't turn out well, and so I only worked when Ella was napping and then after she and Erica went to bed. I was getting really stressed again being the primary caretaker as well as the primary financial provider, yet Erica still was convinced her job was more important since she was on staff at Narconon. Needless to say things were heading south again. Even though we were away from Clearwater, we still weren't away from Scientology. Finally toward the end of October we started Ella in a private preschool in McAlester, and that provided some relief for me and some more interaction with other kids for her.

Continuing to Research

One day I searched for Rena Weinberg online. I came across a comment left on Marty Rathbun's blog that mentioned her name. I read the post and the comments, and then became immersed in it. Over the next several hours I began reading all of the posts and comments over the two-year period since he had started it.

My heart was pounding as I read his and others' personal accounts of what had happened in the church. I finally found that I really wasn't alone. I wasn't crazy in thinking that the people running Scientology were the real lunatics and that they were harming people, lying to them and scamming them out of money. I saw that I wasn't alone in what I had perceived after all.

For some time Marty's blog became my sanctuary and I began leaving an occasional comment under the username "Steve". I also started digging through more comments and finding email addresses for people on various topics, including looking for Rena. I got word from Mike Rinder via Christie Collbran that Rena was last seen in The Hole and that she was likely still there. He saw her personally and was locked in there with her and the others who were imprisoned.

I became more concerned. I sent a message via Facebook to Rena's old assistant, Lisa, who was now out of the Sea Org with a child to see if she knew how to find her. She wrote back, "On Rena I would send a comm to Rena Weinberg, C/O CMO Int 1710 Ivar Ave, LA, CA 90028. Nothing really 'happened' to her she is just doing a project that's pretty long."

My understanding is that was where her mail was screened before receiving it. I wrote a very bland email to get past the screeners. I just let her know that we had moved back to Oklahoma, that we had a daughter, and that Erica was working back at Arrowhead again. I asked her if she could please contact me directly because I needed her personal advice on something. I also told her that Narconon missed her presence. Weeks went by and I didn't get a response.

At the end of October the Senior Case Supervisor from the Kansas City Org, Dan O'Connor, came down to Arrowhead to show the annual IAS event. Dan's previous wife, Arla, had stayed at our house in Clearwater while they were still married, and attested to the state of Clear at Flag the same day as Erica. They wound up getting divorced and Dan married Michael Anzalone's ex-wife Amanda and they had a baby.

Dan asked me before the event if I would get up and say something to the staff about donating to the IAS, because I was the top donor who was present. I told him I didn't feel comfortable doing that because I wasn't going to be donating anymore and wouldn't encourage others too, either. He said he understood and didn't really ask any more questions at that time.

I remember sitting there sort of watching the event and sort of playing with Ella and Dan's baby. I saw some bogus statistics flash up on the screen and the latest Ideal Org pictures, and I was thinking how all of it was horse shit.

Shortly after that day I had gotten a call from Sascha Berlin, and I finally let him have it on the phone. I told him how disgusting it was about the abuse in the Sea Org, about my disapproval of the coerced abortions, about missing executives like Rena and about the fact that almost every single area at Flag has been turned into registration and donation central. I said it was completely screwed up for someone to supposedly be your counselor, then ask you for large sums of money out of obligation to do so and then go back to counseling later, because it created a broken trust and upset and therefore people were not able to achieve the supposed results of the counseling. He disagreed but said he understood where I was coming from. I told him I would not be participating in anything else until I get real answers to my questions. He asked me to email them to him, so I did, but it didn't go any place and I kept "flapping" (causing a stink).

I also spoke to Tracy Lemos after that. She had sent me a packet of information that included some excerpts from Hubbard policies as well as negative information about church members who had signed a list declaring themselves to be Independent Scientologists and denouncing the activities of the official church. She warned told me I better stop reading that stuff online or I would wind up being declared an SP.

Word started to get around Narconon Arrowhead that I was becoming "disaffected" with the church, which was a term the church started using to divide friendships as a step before becoming declared an SP. Erica had told a couple people, who had told a couple people, and so on.

One of her friends was a woman named Joann Baker. Joann had been involved in the church for a very long time and was working at Arrowhead. She said she'd talk to me to try and help and we went out to lunch together one day.

She told me that many people in the early 80's split from the church back when David Miscavige was taking over and Pat Broeker and David Mayo (two church leaders who worked closely with Hubbard) were ousted. She told me that her husband was disaffected and that I should talk to him, which wasn't exactly smart for her to recommend.

She also told me that she lies to people who ask her about the OT III story and Xenu. She said an Arrowhead registrar asked her about it, and even showed her online where it was displayed in Hubbard's own handwriting, and she flatly denied that it was true just to protect the image of the church and to not confuse lower-level Narconon staff. This was a classic example of how Scientologists are taught to think – lie and hide the truth if it hurts the organization.

After lunch I stopped in to see Gary Smith. He told me that I shouldn't put so much attention on the entheta and that it's designed to break up the group. I asked him about Rena and he said he's been wondering about her and asking around as well. He was told by someone at the International Landlord's office that Rena had been in some ethics trouble but that she would be appearing at the upcoming New Year's Event (which didn't happen). He said that he didn't know what was up with Rinder and Rathbun, but that in his mind Miscavige was the one who was really driving everything and needed our support because he was the one who didn't abandon the group.

I wound up driving back home only seeing more of an example of how Scientology was controlling both the upper levels of Narconon and how True Believers such as Gary and Joann were unable to look for themselves. I no longer considered myself one by then.

I finally wound up getting a card back from Rena. All it said was that she was glad to hear we were back in Oklahoma, would like to see my daughter, and that she was "expanding on all 8 dynamics" (she actually underlined that part). She didn't say what she'd been up to. She didn't mention anything about Narconon or ABLE, and she didn't say anything about being able to speak with me.

For me, this confirmed that her communications were being censored and that she was in The Hole and doing the "Int RPF". The RPF stands for the Rehabilitation Project Force and is where Sea Org members are sent to do auditing, training, manual labor and other work. They are cut off from speaking to the outside world and have only minimal contact with friends and family, if any. One of the main tasks done in the RPF is called the False Purpose Rundown (FPRD), which is meant to locate hidden false purposes and evil intentions in different areas of life. On the RPF, it is done on all 8 dynamics as Hubbard defined them. The Int RPF/ The Hole was the worst of the worst, by all first-hand accounts.

The end result of the RPF is a more compliant staff member, willing to carry out any order and willing to endure anything for the benefit of the group, as anything else is deemed a false purpose. This is the most hideous brainwashing technique in all of Scientology, in my opinion. It is how Sea Org members justify so many wrongdoings or even adopt the idea that they are necessary actions to protect the group. They take Hubbard's and Miscavige's words literally and believe they are the only hope for mankind and that there is no room for "namby-pamby bunch of panty-waist dilettantes" (a reference from Hubbard's series of policies written about Keeping Scientology Working). I met several people who had completed the regular RPF in other locations and they were unable to see that committing crimes and defrauding people wasn't okay since they were being done for the benefit of Scientology.

Trying to Get Erica to Look

I posted this on one of my blogs at the end of November 2010, and shared the link on Facebook, too. It was a subtle hint of my continuing discovery.

> I've looked at quite a few subjects lately, both on personal and societal scales, and found myself wondering just when is ignorance bliss and when is it, well, ignorant?
>
> Choosing to take the red or blue capsule a la The Matrix is a choice we have with any subject, really, if we choose. But what if your life seems happier not knowing the full truth? Is it really happier or are you just living a lie?
>
> For example, I love a good burger, steak, grilled chicken breast or a honey-glazed ham, but do I really want to see what goes on at slaughter houses? I mean, I have seen some pictures and have a pretty good idea, but is it necessary to get all the gory details, and if I did, would I still eat meat? Hell, I rarely go fishing because I hate putting the bait on the hook and then hate having to rip the hook out of the fish after they're caught, but I still love seafood.
>
> What about our nation's obsession with prescription drugs -

would people be better off knowing that the drug they've been convinced to take by some clueless doctor, slick salesperson or brilliant marketing scheme is doing less for them then what simple nutritional supplements would do? What about if the drug is actually making them worse? Beyond that, do they really want to know that many of the drug companies know their drugs are causing harm and set aside hundreds of millions to settle lawsuits so that they can still pocket billions of dollars over time, regardless of the human cost in terms of patient side effects including sending droves of people to seek drug rehabilitation help, or even death?

And how about your religion? What if yours really wasn't the only true way to the afterlife, however you believe it to be? What if what your religious texts promise you were nothing but contrived scenes to control masses, or offer uplifting hope for them? I don't think it's bad to believe in something if it's meant to help you live your life better and treat others well, but it would be nice to have a way of knowing the absolute truth about the texts and history without having to simply trust the authority who is handing it down to you, assuming it is unaltered.

In sports, do performance enhancing drug scandals make you question your favorite players? Would it matter to you if most of the athletes were using, or if the leagues changed rules to allow them? Would you stop watching games and competitions if news broke that a large percentage of the players were cheating?

Regarding your kids, would you want to know the details about their sex lives and whether or not they used drugs or engaged in some other type of harmful or illegal activities even if they were always home on time, kept a job, never got in trouble and excelled in their studies?

Finding the man behind the curtain like The Wizard of Oz

can take the wind out of our sails, but in many more situations it can also remove the fear or mystery surrounding the situation.

I believe that the full truth should be made available for all to know, if they choose to know, but they have to be willing to accept and deal with the truth if it is shockingly different from what they thought previously.

There may be a time and a place for everything, and the level of details can vary. I don't think kids have to be traumatized with images of slaughter houses before they decide to have a chicken nugget. It's not entirely necessary for me to know the detailed history of the secretive Federal Reserve before I spend my money. However, children should understand how animals become food, people should understand the realities of our nation's financial structure and we all should get the truth about what we put into our body, about our governments and our religions.

Needless to say, that didn't go over well for my Scientologist friends who read it, as any doubt or questioning of Hubbard and Scientology are viewed as "enemy lines".

The Basics were supposed to be unadulterated LRH, as were the Ideal Org campaigns, but many discrepancies were found. One was the fact that at least one of Hubbard's lectures warning about a dictator taking over Scientology had been edited. They also changed the entire meaning of what an Ideal Org is supposed to be.

These were some of the things discussed on Marty's blog and elsewhere. Another thing brought up was a Hubbard lecture that said that the day Scientology started putting emphasis on buildings is the day that rebel Scientologists should essentially overthrow the leadership.

I pulled out the transcript of that lecture to show to Erica one night after we had been arguing heavily. She read it and said, "Did you get this off one of your black PR sites? I don't care about anything they have to say".

"But it's LRH," I pleaded.

"I don't care. I don't want to hear any of that suppressive bullshit. It's entheta. You're fucking suppressive."

I couldn't believe it. I wasn't even able to get her to look at anything for herself and examine it against what was happening.

She had started communicating more with people at Flag about me. She was basically turning me in for having become disaffected. Our fights got worse.

Around this time I decided I wanted to sell all of my FSM websites. I wanted to be done with Narconon and Scientology and move on to do other things. I started shopping around for prices, knowing that I could have gotten more if I went outside the fold to regular business circles.

"You can't do that," Erica told me. "You have to sell them to stay in the Narconon network at least."

"Why not? I asked. They're my sites, I built them, and it's better for our family if I can get more money for them."

"You're so off-purpose. That's fucking suppressive."

I couldn't believe how ridiculous she sounded, and I actually laughed at it, but then she leapt from the couch at me. I tried to block her swing as her fist connected to my shoulder. I bent over and turned away as she pushed me and swung again.

"You're the worst husband ever," she screamed, "I hope you fucking die!"

She stormed off into the bedroom as I was in a bit of shock. Here the person who was supposed to have my back, and who I thought I had done everything I could to support was saying that to me. I was crushed.

I went into my home office and got on the computer again, which was one of the only places that I felt comfortable anymore. A few minutes later she came in and apologized to me. She said she just wished I would go down to Flag and get it all sorted out. I told her I wanted nothing to do with Flag anymore. She walked out, silently this time, and closed the door behind her.

That night I wrote this:

The Parting Sky

Here it is
The calm before the storm
I can't explain
Why my heart feels torn

On the one hand it's love
Filled with memories
There's nothing you've done
To make me wanna leave

You deserve all the best
And what you want is not me
I know you're hurt
But soon you will see

The clouds on the horizon
Random shapes creating
All the while drifting
Effortlessly explaining

And after the lightning
The wind and the rain
The sun will come out
And shine on you again

Your persistence I adore
Damn, you deserve more
Gone will be the fighting
And relief will wash ashore

So here's to a new life
Where we both can fulfill
Our chosen directions
Each other at the wheel

But we will always have

This beautiful girl
For together we shape
And protect her world

So let's make a pact
To help each other out
On the road to the future
We'll make it no doubt

I wished there was a way for her to see, but she had clearly chosen Scientology over me, and so only another Scientologist who would bend to her wishes was going to make her happy. I was miserable and couldn't go on. Beaten down and giving up, but I didn't show it to her then.

Venturing Back to Clearwater

I decided I just needed space. Our home in Georgia was empty again and it was a place for me to go and get a way. I also missed being in the home and the life that we had back then – back before going to Clearwater.

One night in December I told her I thought we needed to separate. I had typed up an agreement for her to sign, though she didn't want to hear it. She broke down. She couldn't understand and was yelling in front of Ella. She then wanted me to call my mom and tell her that I was leaving, to say it right in front of her. After that she called her mom to tell her the same thing - that I was the one leaving. Technically, yes, I was physically driving to give us relief from the fighting, but in reality she had separated from me long before when she had chosen to listen to the church and not even hear what I had to say. It was awful, and all three of us were crying.

Erica and Ella went to bed, and I slept on the couch that night as usual. I felt so lost, alone and hurt and didn't know how to even get her to see what was happening. No doubt she felt the same way because she thought she was losing me to the dark side.

The next morning I took Ella to school and told her I would be back in a few days. Erica and I had both calmed down a bit and I decided that I was just going to go every other week. I also wrote her a check for half our savings account.

One day when I was in Georgia I got a call from Bob Adams. He had since moved from ABLE to become a VP for the Church of Scientology International and was posted in OSA. I politely asked him where Rena was and that I had been trying to locate her for quite some time. He said he wasn't entirely sure and that maybe I should ask her husband. I said that I already did contact Brian, but that he said he couldn't tell me.

Bob then awkwardly changed the topic and wanted to know how I was doing. I was very suspicious that he would call me out of the blue like that after all that was going with me. I wound up determining that he wasn't aware because he was too busy on other things. He then launched into an explanation of how the church was working to get some kind of outreach program going in California and it needed support. That was it. He was calling and asking me for money. The Vice President of the Church of Scientology International had been reduced to making donation solicitation calls to people like me. That solidly confirmed (as if any more confirmation was really necessary) that their primary focus at the top was to acquire as much money as possible. I of course told him that I didn't have any money to donate and we ended the call.

Over the next few weeks I spent a lot of time researching what to do with selling my websites, and told the guy who was working for me that I wanted to get rid of them. He was a Scientologist and wanted to keep them in the Narconon network as well. He said he wanted an opportunity to put together an offer, and I agreed to not sell until I had his offer.

I also spent a lot of time watching videos of interviews with Scientologists who have left, including the one that Mark Bunker posted of actor Jason Beghe. He said a lot of things that hit home for me - things that I thought but was terrified of voicing because of what happens to you if you say them while inside the church. The more I read and examined, the more I wanted to have nothing to do with Scientology at all. One other particularly telling sign was a series of clips from a *60 Minutes* broadcast about the Scientology. It talked about the arrests after the FBI raid in the late 70's and how church members then just turned away from the fact that the organization they supported had infiltrated the government, framed author Paulette Cooper and committed other crimes. That same piece showed church President Heber Jentzsch saying, "Scientology is the only road to total Freedom." I finally saw that the behavior I was experiencing from current church members was nothing new.

When I was in Oklahoma we hardly talked and all my clothes had been moved into the guest room. We were stuck. When I was in Georgia we would fight on the phone. I told her I was willing to be the bad guy, to take the blame for leaving if she was afraid of what other people thought, as she knew neither one of us were happy. She told me that she just wished I'd go down to Flag and talk to someone. I was in Georgia at the time, less than eight hours' drive away. I thought for a second and finally said, "Okay. I'll go."

"Really?!" she said excitedly.

"Yes, but you have to promise me something. If I get declared you have to promise me that you will never try and keep me from seeing Ella."

"Ok, I promise," she agreed.

We both contacted people at Flag that night saying that I would be coming down. There were people from the Chaplain's office that I was supposed to meet with.

I drove down on Friday, January 21st, 2011. On my way into town I met with the Scientologist who wanted to buy my websites. His deal was considerably less than what I had been offered, but I was trying to show a measure of good faith and agreed to sell them to him at that price, in weekly payments over two years rather than getting the money up front. It was also way less than what they originally were worth because they had been penalized in Google and were under-performing, but they were fully aware of this, as was the buyer who had offered much more and the broker who had quoted me a selling price.

The first night I stayed at JT's house. After all, he'd been my friend for many years. The church told him I couldn't stay there and told me I needed to get a hotel, so on Saturday I checked in to the La Quinta. It was stupid. They knew I had read a lot online and didn't want me to communicate anything to JT, which I hadn't intended to unless they refused to answer my questions. Nonetheless, I went over to the hotel.

On Monday afternoon we had the contract signed to sell the sites. I trusted this guy and didn't have an attorney look over the contract, though I should have and missed some key points in it that were later used against me. It turned out to be financially devastating, as I was planning to use the money to make a full transition into other areas of interest.

Later that afternoon two people from the Chaplain's office at Flag came to my hotel room. We sat and talked for over an hour, including about things such as the physical abuse, coerced abortions, alteration of materials, missing staff, OT's and former senior staff who have left the church. For every objection or question they either had some bullshit PR answer for me that was obvious or tried to show me a reference from Hubbard that was pulled and often used out of context.

I confronted them on something from the Truth Rundown series of articles about a large group of Sea Org members being marched into the pond at the Int Base, fully clothed, and then sent back to work completely soaked and cold. One of the women, Sharon, said that sounded a bit far-fetched. I then pointed out that Tommy Davis was actually recorded admitting to that happening. After that she said, "Well, you know LRH was the one who instituted over boarding back on the Apollo as a form of discipline. It's not something new." I was pretty shocked that she thought it seemed unbelievable at first and then defended the action because Hubbard used to have people tossed into the ocean as punishment and then retrieved. At the end, I told them that it was pretty pointless, because they weren't honest with me about much at all.

They said they'd like me to get a metered interview, but I said I had already been there for a few days and I was leaving, although I did agree to come back in about two weeks. Erica tried to plead with me to stay, but I was so sick of being there already and started to have a taste of freedom.

HAVE YOU TOLD ALL?

On the way out of town I got a call from Sara, who was in charge of the Chaplain's office. She also pleaded with me to stay, and we got in an argument over the phone, but I kept driving. I had given them a chance, but still assured her I would be back in a couple of weeks. I also knew that they had a tendency to sequester people and make them stay for long periods of time, but I was determined to not let that happen.

At the end of January, I posted a song that I had written about Ella right after she was born. I really wanted everything to work out.

> When I think of you all I do is smile
> I'm comin' home, daydreamin' all the while
> 'Cause being away is tugging at my heart
> All these miles between us are tearing me apart
>
> I remember that day when you came into this world
> There you were, a perfect little girl
> Your mother and I - full of hope and nerves, oh boy
> That's when I first had these wondrous tears of joy
>
> I hear that thunder, and the cool spring rain
> Bringing new life, and washing away the pain
> It's all around us, like a gift from Him above
> So innocent and pure - it's unconditional love
> So many things remind me of that time
> When I first saw that little girl of mine
>
> And being away is tugging at my heart
> All this miles between us are tearing me apart
>
> I remember that day when you came into this world
> And there you were, a perfect little girl
> You're mother and I so full of hope and nerves, oh boy
> That's when I first had these wondrous tears of joy
>
> The last time I saw you was only two weeks ago
> But each time I come home I see how much you've grown

I can't explain the feeling that's inside
Being your Daddy brings me so much pride
Your precious face, and the dimple in your cheek
Your big blue eyes watching me, the guidance that you seek

So many things to come, seeing you grow up
Walking and talking, and getting your first pup
Fifty years together doesn't seem like enough time
To spend my days with this little girl of mine
That's why I quit this long and lonely road today
To be close to you and watch you laugh and play

Cause being away was tugging at my heart
All those miles between us were tearing me apart

I remember that day when you came into this world
And there you were, a perfect little girl
Now here I am, to be with you and say
I'm so thankful for each and every day

Sure enough, I did arrive two weeks later. This time they were more prepared for me. I went in to see Daniel, the MAA. While I was waiting, I wasn't allowed to be out of anyone's sight. They were afraid I would be spouting information to other people there. I told Daniel that I had email contact with Marty Rathbun and a few others. After the interview he reported this to OSA, and said that I would have an interview after lunch. He was ordered to not let me out of his sight, and actually had to eat lunch with me. I asked him if this was the case and he said yes, but also that the person who was supposed to meet with me was high up and I needed to be available the moment she arrives.

Another hour or so later she hadn't arrived. Daniel came out and said that she would meet me the next day at my hotel room, and I said I was fine with that.

The 6-Hour "Interview"

The next day a woman named Kathy True showed up at my hotel with a young man who was also in the Sea Org. She was carrying an e-meter and introduced herself. He went out to the car, which was parked just outside the room, and waited for her there. She asked if she could do a metered interview, and I said yes, but that I was also told she would be able to answer my questions. She said she could do that, and would answer them after we finished the interview. Kathy works for OSA at Flag, so she was a trained liar.

We proceeded with the interview, but it wasn't really an interview. It turned out to be a thinly-veiled sec check, with a list of prepared questions wanting to know things about my present and past as well as who I'd spoken to, what I said and what my plans were.

She was probing for my crimes, as they're told anyone critical of Scientology has crimes. She was asking about my sex life and if I had cheated on my wife, she asked if I'd been getting drunk or high, she asked if I stole things, lied to anyone, etc. I hadn't done anything wrong though, except for investigating and going against the status quo of the Scientologist sheeple.

The probing questions continued for hours, literally. At one point I told her I was done answering her questions until she answered mine, as she promised she would do. I told her it seemed like she was lying to me. "Have you ever lied to anyone?" she asked. L. Ron Hubbard said that criminals accuse others of things they are doing themselves, so she assumed I was lying about something since I was getting upset about the situation.

She then asked me how many times I commented on Marty's blog. I told her I thought it was a handful. She started asking questions about a different time period, inferring that I was lying to her. OSA reads Marty's blog daily and tries to track down who the various screen names are for people who haven't publicly identified themselves yet. There had been another commenter who used "Steve" as his handle several months earlier, though I was able to prove it wasn't me by some of the information and locations he provided in his comments. It turns out that I had made a total of 18 comments from November 2010 through

January 2011. She pulled out the stack they had printed off to show me. Some were a couple simple agreements, while others were more involved.

One of my comments said that I thought Miscavige needed to be hauled off in handcuffs and put in an orange jumpsuit or something to that effect. This was appalling to them, and was apparently more blasphemous than any other comment I had made. I told her I still felt that way if what I read was true. I could have stated that L. Ron Hubbard was the devil incarnate and it wouldn't have been as bad to her as my statement about Miscavige in handcuffs. We had several heated exchanges about the state of the church and what was going on both internally and in the public eye, such as Tommy Davis lying about disconnection on CNN, etc.

I started to get really hungry, and took a break to grab a burrito from Chipotle around the corner. I ate quickly and came back, eager to finish up and get to my part so that I could get the answers I was promised.

When I came back I forwarded her the email exchanges I had with four people who had left the church, again as a sign of good faith and honesty. There was no attempt to rat on anyone and there was nothing more revealing in them than what had been publicly posted online.

OSA had gone through all of my ethics files and counseling folders to find people I was connected to and situations I was involved in before, whether good or bad. Kathy was there to do a thorough probing.

Kathy also questioned me as to why I felt like I needed to protect my parents from the church. I tried to explain how every time they came to a church for any kind of service, that registrars would hunt them down and try and extract large sums of money from them, so I believed I had to try and keep the regges away. I thought it was my duty to protect them from the wolves, but Kathy didn't understand because a real Scientologist would want others to donate all they could, in her mind.

Another hour later we finally started to get to the point of wrapping up, and she was doing a variation of end rudiments on me, asking if I failed to tell anything, if I only told a half-truth about something, if I had told all, or if I was still withholding anything. Finally it was determined I had been completely honest about everything, which I had been.

I then asked her if it was my turn. She said, "Well I can't trust you with that information now that I know you've taken it this far."

I was livid on the inside, but calmly told her that she just proved my suspicions correct. I had just endured six hours of hell and put everything out in the open under the guise that I was finally going to get someone high up enough to level with me about what was really going on behind the scenes and what was being done to fix it. Boy was I naive. What a fucking joke.

The next day I got a call from Kathy saying to meet her in front of the Clearwater Bank building on the corner of Ft. Harrison Ave. and Cleveland St. downtown around 9 PM.

I sent her a text when I arrived. The large green door opened behind me and she summoned me inside, which was a large, open room with a single desk in it and perfectly polished marble floors. She ushered me over to an adjoining conference room where she introduced me to Marion Pouw from CMO Int, which stands for Commodore's Messengers Org and used to be staffed with Hubbard's personal messengers. I extended my hand during the introduction, but Marion just looked back at me and said, "Have a seat." She made it clear she wasn't there to be friendly and was using a form of manipulation by showing the upper hand right off the bat.

"You're in serious trouble," she exclaimed, "Do you know that?"

She pulled out a file that had information about me in it and some Hubbard references.

"We don't usually give people in your position much of a chance, but somehow you were able to get me and Kathy sitting here willing to work with you. So what's it going to be, are we wasting our time here or are you going to work with us?"

"It depends on what you're going to ask me to do," I replied honestly.

She opened the folder and pointed to a section of one of the policies that spoke of suppressive acts against the church, indicating what I had done and what situation I was in.

There are steps written out that someone can take who was declared an SP by the church to be able to rejoin the group, labeled A through E. It is often referred to as an A to E program. She asked me to read over it, and I did.

"You're starting right now. You're going to get through the first two steps tonight. We're not going to issue any official declaration on you, but you need to know the severity of your position within the church. Of course if you don't cooperate then we will issue the goldenrod."

Goldenrod is the color of paper that ethics orders are written on in Scientology and Narconon. She was letting me know that if I didn't comply I would be cut off from all friends and family on the spot. Reasoning with them at that point wasn't an option, so I went with the self-preservation instinct to go along with them at that time for fear of something worse happening.

I sure as hell didn't appreciate the accusatory tone in her voice, and I told her that I never had my questions answered about the abortions, violence, financial fraud, bullshit statistics at events, and more. She started to argue with me and defend the Sea Org's importance and David Miscavige, specifically. I asked about Rena Weinberg and she said that she was at the Int Base after all and had seen her recently. I asked her why I wasn't allowed to communicate with Rena privately and directly.

"Rena is a senior-level officer in the Sea Org," Marion snapped, "she's not just available to anyone."

"I considered her a friend," I barked back, "I didn't realize she wasn't allowed to have friends."

They continued on to tell me that I would be able to work directly with them and not have to go through normal channels. It was a verbal declare, which is highly against even church policy. Instead I believe they thought I could wind up being a pawn for them, since I had been so honest and showed them my communications, in being able to find out identities of others who were distancing themselves from the church and attacking David Miscavige.

The first step of the A to E program included not doing the things that one was supposedly guilty of doing before. The second one was to write up a form of public announcement of what was done, denouncing those actions or statements and how it would be fixed.

I wrote down what I did. I admitted doing it but still felt it was the correct thing to do as they were obviously lying and committing real crimes. I showed it to Kathy, but she sent me back to add more to it. She said she wanted it to be as detailed as possible and wanted me to specifically mention bad things about Marty Rathbun. I was told it would be posted on a website that was built especially for others that were in a similar situation as I was regarding having doubts about the church.

We went through an additional three more changes before I finally wrote it the way Kathy and Marion wanted it written.

Another step as part of the program was to redo any courses and training that I had previously done at my own expense. I told them I wasn't willing to do that. Then they said maybe I just had to redo a couple or maybe complete the entire Basics books and lectures series. Again, I said I wasn't willing to do that, but was just told that I could deal with that later.

After that Kathy sat down with me and said, "I think you have a misunderstood about what LRH wrote in *Dianetics* about abortions." She had a copy of the book and I welcomed the challenge. "It's not that we advocate them, but it is up to each individual woman if she wants to have the child or not. Plus, they signed an agreement with the understanding that they were not to have children, so just the irresponsible act of getting pregnant would be considered out-ethics in the Sea Org."

I couldn't believe she was so stupid to defend coerced abortions. I told her that I wasn't a woman and so I didn't feel I had the right to take a stance of judgment either way, but that I certainly wasn't in favor of it being repeatedly condoned, suggested or coerced. I then showed in her in *Dianetics* what Hubbard wrote - she was the one who had the misunderstanding. The only way to really reason with a Scientologist, especially a Sea Org member, is to use Hubbard's own written or recorded words. They cannot have independent thought outside of that on much other than mundane daily activities.

I also had to propose an amends project that seemed acceptable to them and send to the International Justice Chief (IJC).

After this was accomplished and they felt they got their product with me, they sat me back down in the conference room and showed me a propaganda DVD that the church had created against the Anonymous movement. It painted the entire group out to be scary hackers - cyber terrorists who pull pranks and call in death threats. After the short video I was shown pictures of former church executives who had been spotted with members of Anonymous, who were easily identified by the Guy Fawkes masks. The idea was to put it in my head that the people I had started to communicate with were somehow evil.

I left the meeting shortly after midnight, glad that I had escaped with my connections still somewhat intact. I believed I would be able to somehow make it go away, and that there was a shot at reasoning with them down the road, especially since there was no official record of the clandestine meeting.

I called Erica and let her know what happened. She said I could go to Dallas for a few months and complete all of my courses right away. I said there was no way I was doing that and to back off, but she kept on. I said I was tired and that we would talk about it when I got home.

Trying to Reconcile

When I got back to Oklahoma I told Erica that I really wanted to give the marriage another shot. In her mind I was now cooperating with the church and she thought that I would eventually get back in good standing with them and return for more auditing again. That was why she was pushing so heavily for me to get started on my courses full-time.

This became a new problem, as well as how quickly or slowly I was moving on my amends project. She was designated as my primary contact, and that I wasn't supposed to communicate with people at Narconon anymore or other church members either, yet I hadn't been declared.

I started getting very frustrated with this, not only the fact of

Erica pushing me, but because Kathy was calling in to Narconon Arrowhead as well as Narconon International and telling people what I had done, instructing them to stay away until I completed my A to E program.

Erica and I had several more arguments about this, and I was emailing Kathy about it, as was she. In fact, she was reporting me to them every time we fought about the church or I disagreed with stuff. I had gone back and reviewed a Hubbard policy and demanded that I get a Committee of Evidence (Comm Ev), as the policy clearly stated that if my contributions to the group far outweighed any perceived crimes, that I should be absolved.

Once again Erica was angry with me. "You just need to do the fucking program and get on with it," she said.

I tried to explain the position I was in, but it was impossible for her to even see because she still wouldn't even consider finding out either what I had discovered or what I had actually done. All she did was take their word. I stopped doing my amends and said that per policy I deserved a Comm Ev. I had a conversation with Kathy and Marion and told them it was bullshit what they did and that I wasn't going to play along with it any more. They couldn't argue with the Comm Ev policy, so they said ok and turned it over to a senior Ethics person at Flag.

A couple weeks later my Comm Ev was scheduled, so I drove back down to Clearwater in March.

I arrived at Flag and sat in the MAA reception room after 9:00 and was ushered into another room. There were four senior ethics people there and one OSA member. I knew it was a stacked deck but I thought that I had enough evidence on my side and LRH references to back up my position. I stated repeatedly that I just wanted it to be dropped and to let me go on with my life. There is an audio recording of the whole thing that they have, per the Comm Ev policy.

They actually agreed that my contributions outweighed whatever acts I had supposedly committed, and I pled guilty to all but one of them, thinking that would show them I was looking for some type of resolution. The secretary also admitted to the fact that Hubbard's materials were altered, specifically the lecture about one man taking over Scientology, but was told that there was a group of people whose job it was to review Hubbard's material for possible out-PR points, and that was why it was removed (though the question about interracial sex was left in the Joburg?).

I was asked if I would comply with any recommendations that the Comm Ev had that included auditing or training and I said no, that I just wanted to be left alone and after what I had been through and witnessed up to that point I had no intentions of returning to Scientology. However, I was willing to go away quietly back then if they would leave me alone.

At that point the Comm Ev ended. It had only lasted about an hour. I crashed at my hotel and then took off first thing in the morning. I thought I was successful in stating my case and was actually eager to move on with my life.

Changing Directions

Since I wasn't doing rehab referrals anymore for Narconon, I had decided that I was going to make a documentary film with interviews of addiction professionals that had alternative viewpoints. I started making contacts and wanted to capture the interviews over the next few months. My goal at the time wasn't to promote any particular type of rehab or form of treatment, but instead to forward the idea that all addicts didn't have to be labeled as having an incurable disease for life.

I had contacted Eric Sherman again in LA and got a recommendation from him for an affordable videographer - a former graduate film school student of his, who had no connection to Narconon or Scientology.

I searched outside of the Narconon arena, but found quite a bit of resistance from people in the addiction treatment field, even if alternative-minded, due to my previous associations with Narconon. I found some willing to speak to me, but only off the record. They were supportive of the project but still skeptical of my connections. I also had some who initially agreed to be interviewed but then backed out afterwards. Others simply didn't reply or they had no interest.

I felt hampered but was determined to still get the project completed, and so I wound up including interviews with people still connected to Narconon or Scientology. I had no intention of forwarding their movements. I simply wanted people to discuss certain topics on camera. I wound up with about half and half in terms of association.

One of my more intriguing and professional interviewees had a PhD in psychology who brought my attention to the National Epidemiological Survey of Alcoholism and Related Conditions (NESARC). This study showed that three quarters of people who fit the classification as having alcohol abuse or dependency between the ages of 18 to 25 no longer fall in those categories later in life, whether they went to treatment or not. There is a lot of validity to simply maturing out of poor drinking habits and behaviors. Another thing I've learned is to really look at the severity of symptoms, and that it is impossible to lump any substance abusers or addicts into one category, definition or diagnosis.

Getting Divorced

I was outside washing my car one day when Erica came out to talk to me. She looked at me and said with disdain that she wanted a divorce and she wanted me to leave immediately. She had gone on my computer and looked at my web history. I looked at her, didn't see an ounce of independent thought in her eyes, and decided not to fight anymore after so many attempts to get her to look at what was really happening. She had fully taken their side and wasn't even going to hear about or look at what I found.

She asked me to pack a bag and leave right away. I calmly went inside and did so, and told Ella that I had to go out of town for a couple days for a meeting. Erica had a work trip to Arizona planned for later that week and Ella and I were going to go to Georgia during that time, so I told her I'd pick her up and to make sure she's ready for the vacation.

In the next two days I found a small duplex to rent and put a deposit down right away to reserve it. I was going to be moving in on the 15th of April, less than two weeks from Ella's 4th birthday. I was crushed, but didn't see any other alternative. Scientology had fully taken over my wife and had continued to rip apart my life.

After getting back from our respective trips, we tried to make the change happen as gradually as possible for Ella. She was already used to me sleeping on the couch and going back to work in my office after she want to bed, but the difference was my office was no longer in the house.

I would pick her up from preschool, make dinner for her and play with her. Then I would leave when it was time for her to go to bed. The first few weeks this was agonizing, as Ella would cling to me when I tried to leave and even followed me out to my car several times in tears. I spent many nights crying myself to sleep. This little girl didn't deserve to have her family ripped apart by an evil outside influence that she couldn't understand. All she knew was that her parents fought a lot and that it was better for her to not be around constant fighting.

At the end of the month was her birthday, and to try and make things a little better for her I stayed at the house and my parents came in town as well. While several people from Narconon came with their kids, there was no discussion about my situation and I had very little interaction with them. For me, it was all about my daughter having a good time, and nothing else.

In May Bobby Newman was in town to visit from Hawaii. He had been such a good friend for a number of years. He came over to my rental and we had a conversation about my standing within the group. He said that Dan Manson, the president of Narconon Vista Bay in Northern California who was on OT VII, had told him to stay away from me. Bobby said that he knew I was a good guy and had hoped there was some way to get it all sorted out.

I explained about the recent Comm Ev in Clearwater and that I had not heard anything back since then. I did not go into any detail about my upsets, but did make it clear that I wasn't willing to do what they were asking of me, and if they can't see what is happening then that is not something I wanted to be involved with anymore. I also said that I had no problems with what anyone wanted to believe or practice as long as it wasn't harmful. He said, "Well, you know if you do ever get officially declared then I'm going to have to disconnect. I have too much invested in this whole thing. I hope you understand."

I absolutely understood. I understood the amount of undue influence Scientology and Narconon place on people, and I was in the middle of trying to break free from that influence. I knew that any real attempt to convince him otherwise would just result in more reports written on me to the church.

We went back to the previous schedule for the month of May. Then at the beginning of June, Erica had already planned to go to Flag for the summer to take a couple courses and Ella was going to go to a summer camp there. I had begun my filming and made plans to take several trips over the summer travel schedule to see Ella in Florida. Before they left, Erica had filed the divorce papers that we had agreed to at the time.

11 DISCONNECTION HITS

Erica and Ella had already arrived in FL and one of my first visits was right after filming interviews in Albany, NY and Chatham, NJ. I couldn't wait to see Ella. It had been just under a couple of weeks, which was by that time the most we had ever spent apart from each other. It wasn't a long trip, but very meaningful for both of us. I wanted to reassure her that no matter what I would always be there for her even if it couldn't be every day – that I would always find a way to see her despite the obstacles.

The next trip was at the end of June, right after Father's Day. I had gone by a local car dealership where I bought my car. I wanted to trade in my car and get another manual transmission. I had gotten an automatic (the only automatic I bought for myself) so that Erica could drive it, but really missed shifting gears. The dealership had erroneously ordered three cars in a particular model I was interested in, and made an impulsive decision to buy one of them after driving it. The car was/is way out of my price range, but what can I say – I felt the need for some comfort.

Then I finished up my last day of filming on June 23rd. The next day I got a call from the Flag Justice Chief, who was a girl named Cara Golashesky in her mid-twenties. I agreed to meet her at the parking lot in front of the Clearwater public library, and proceeded to follow her to her office, which was in an obscure place on Fort Harrison Ave. behind the Clearwater Bank building that the church owned.

"I wanted to go over the findings and recommendations of your Comm Ev with you," she said, as she handed me the sheets of goldenrod paper.

I read it over. The committee found me guilty on all charges and recommended that I be officially declared a Suppressive Person. Cara agreed and signed off on it.

I was stunned. It had been months since my Comm Ev and I thought it was behind me. I tried to argue with her about the whole thing, but she said the only thing she wanted to discuss at that point was my A to E program, which she said she would help me complete. I told her that I wasn't interested in doing that, so it was a waste of time.

I left Cara's office and called Erica and tried to explain what had just happened. She talked to me like I was some lesser human being, full of disdain. "How could you let this happen?" she said. "All you had to do was finish you're A to E before and this wouldn't have happened."

"You don't get it," I replied, "and I guess you never will." I hung up the phone and I cried. I was uncertain what would happen at that point regarding Ella. The marriage was already over, but I vowed to not lose my daughter to the church as well.

After spending a couple days with Ella, I drove back to Oklahoma. On the way I called JT, Bobby Newman and David Morris to let them know. All three of them said they had to disconnect from me, but they still considered me a friend and they hoped it would work out. When I returned back to McAlester I got a new tattoo of symbols that were supposed to represent freedom and prosperity. I resolved to make sure that everything would be resolved in the end.

Within a couple days word had spread around the Scientology and Narconon communities who knew me that I was declared an SP. I remember sitting on Facebook one night, refreshing my browser every few minutes, and watching the number of friends tick downward. Representatives from the church had called some of my friends and told them I had been declared and that they should cut all ties with me as well as unfriend me on Facebook. They also notified their secret team of "Facebook Police" to start tracking down church members who were connected to me on the social networking site and notifying them to do the same.

Within 24 hours more than a hundred people had unfriended me, which sounds really lame when you look back on it, but at the time what I saw were dozens of people shutting me out of their lives without even asking me what happened. They just blindly followed orders like the sheeple they were.

The same was done at Narconon centers. Staff were told of my SP declare and ordered to not communicate with me. Within a week, about 90 percent of the people in my life disconnected from me without an explanation. I still have the e-mail from Gary Smith stating he was going to show my declare to staff at Arrowhead. He claimed it was only going to be the Scientologist staff, but many more were told and people I used to hang out with could no longer play golf with me and we couldn't hang out with our kids together anymore, whether they considered themselves Scientologists or not.

I spent the next month or more working on film edits and traveling back and forth between Oklahoma and Florida. During this time Erica met another guy, named Oliver, who of course was a Scientologist. I wrote a petition to Scientology's International Justice Chief to have my declare order dropped, but it was denied and referred back to the Flag Justice Chief, so I sent it to her.

Soon Ella finished her summer camp in August and I went to pick her up. We drove from Florida to Georgia to see my family for a few days, and then headed home to Oklahoma. Erica was still working on her Scientology courses, naturally, and stayed in Clearwater longer.

Ella started back at her preschool and I took care of her for another three weeks. I stayed with her at the house, but went to my rental to work during the day. At one point, Ella asked me if we could have some people over from Narconon so she could play with their kids at our house. I told her that we couldn't, but was unable to explain why. "Is it because they're mad at you?" she innocently asked.

"Yes, they think I did something wrong, but I didn't," I replied.

"Well you could just tell them," she said, matter-of-factly.

"I would, but they won't listen," was my solemn response

before changing the subject.

From that point on she knew that if she wanted to play with any of the other kids that only her mom could be with her. How cruel is that? How is a four year old girl supposed to understand that?

The Divorce is Finalized

Erica's cousin had a wedding in Ohio toward the end of September and she was going to drive from Florida straight up there. Her mother flew down to Dallas to bring Ella up to Pennsylvania for a few days and then meet Erica at the wedding.

I decided to head to Nashville for a night to meet my dad and attend a concert. On my way there, I got a call from Erica. "I just wanted to let you know that the judge signed off and everything is done," she said. Just over nine years later, the same judge who signed our marriage certificate also signed our divorce decree. I remember standing in the crowd at the concert fighting back tears.

When they returned from Ohio, the next few months consisted of roughly the same schedule. I would pick up Ella from school at 4 PM each day. We would play, do activities, eat dinner and hang out until about 8:30, and then I would bring her to Erica. She'd get ready for bed, get up and go to school in the morning, and do it all over again. I would have her every Sunday all day and Erica had her every Saturday all day.

This worked out well for me because I actually got to spend more waking time with Ella and see her six days per week.

During the day I spent time trying to market my video and submitting it to film festivals for consideration. I also continued researching more of the history of Scientology and L. Ron Hubbard

Erica and I continued to argue whenever the subject of the church came up. "You know that if you don't handle your declare that I will have to disconnect from you completely," she told me. "If you would just get back into good standing then we wouldn't have any more problems. You can go about your life and I'll go about mine and we can even be at Ella's birthdays together."

I told her I had submitted a petition, but that I was never going to do my A to E program. Either they dropped the declare or not, and that I had tried to contact Cara regarding my petition for it to be cancelled.

On October 26, 2011 Gabriel Graves died at Narconon Arrowhead, of what was later to be deemed an unidentified cause. I was called that week by an FSM for Arrowhead who told me about the situation. I was in shock. I couldn't believe that they had someone die in the program, as there had been no student deaths that I knew of the entire time I was a student at or directly employed by Narconon in Oklahoma.

By then there was Gabriel at Arrowhead, but it was also revealed that Kayse Werninck had also passed at a local hospital due to alleged negligence at Narconon Arrowhead on March 3, 2009. Kayse's perents had filed suit against Narconon and it was settled pretty quietly. I never saw any media or other reports of her death until people started looking at court records after Gabriel's death.

During this time Erica continued to date Oliver from Clearwater. I had a chance to meet him, briefly, and he seemed like a pretty decent guy. Soon she told me she wanted to put the house up for sale and move back to Clearwater.

In November the *St. Petersburg Times* came out with another series of articles on Scientology and included interviews with more former members. It was called The Money Machine and detailed how money-driven the entire operation really was, with specific amounts that were in the hundreds of millions from Flag. I could completely relate and saw how so many other people were being affected like I was and walking away.

I still read all of Marty Rathbun's posts on his blog, but I also started reading every other story that hit about Scientology online, especially Tony Ortega's blog. I also kept up my research and read more about OT VII Rex Fowler's murder conviction in Colorado, the history behind Lisa McPherson's death at Flag, earlier accounts from people who left before Miscavige took over, Hubbard's connection to the occult, other intimidation tactics and criminal acts under his watch and more. I began to realize how it really wasn't just a church management issue, but that despite any good that came out of Scientology, it's inherent flaws were truly the result of its founder.

We got through the Holidays and were actually pretty cordial together. Then on New Year's Eve I received an email from Debbie Cook, the former Captain of Flag Land Base, as did approximately 10,000 other current and former Scientologists. It outlined her upsets and disagreements with David Miscavige and the direction that Scientology had taken. It also said that Scientology now had more than a billion dollars in reserve cash. I remember being very excited, because I thought this was something that could hopefully wake up enough people involved in the church to bring about reform. While it absolutely had a substantial impact, and still continues to do so, it wasn't the revealing windfall I had hoped for.

Moving Back to Georgia

By the end of January 2012 we were set to move. The tenants had moved out of my house in Georgia and we had arranged time and travel schedules. I was prepared to move to Florida, but Erica said she was willing to do whatever it took for me to not be near her, and we carved out large chunks of time for Ella to be in Georgia in order for me to agree.

Ella and I drove out in a U-Haul on the 22nd of January and spent nearly a week together in Georgia. Erica and her mom drove from Oklahoma and stopped in on the 28th. They picked up Ella and dropped off Oliver the dog. It was now the second time we had moved somewhere and left an empty house that I had to pay for, but I was grateful to be back in Georgia and close to my family and old friends again since basically none of my friends in Oklahoma or Florida would talk to me any more.

Erica again told me that she'd like me to handle my situation with the church so that our communications didn't have to be limited. I told her the only chance was for my petition to get approved to cancel it and have a truce called because I had no intentions of ever being involved with them again. She reminded me that if my SP declare didn't get lifted she would eventually have to completely disconnect from me.

She had limited talking to me directly about anything, unless absolutely necessary and only involving Ella since she got back to Clearwater and pressure from the church was put back on her. A simple argument about where to meet regarding time with Ella turned into "fuck off and die" and "don't ever talk to me again" via text.

A few weeks later in early March she was trying to change the schedule and reduce the amount of time Ella and I spent together. She claimed it was because of school commitments, but Ella was still only 4 and I paid the tuition for the private school. As I pointed those out she got furious and hung up on me.

In a series of texts after that I tried to tell her about Debbie Cook's lawsuit and testimony. She of course wouldn't hear any of it, and wrote back, "Ur the worst person I have ever met u literally make me sick. U lost ur wife friends group and still try to blame others truly pathetic Luke. Ur disgusting u make me sick...And I never want to be apart of any of the shit you spew. I don't care I am happy and I will never change my mind. Ever so don't even try I chose my side a long time ago...Y dont u just die? Ur a cancer. U make me sick. Die seriously just die. Ur a real piece of shit. Ur suppressive. I will never want to hear your disgusting shit u read on the Internet."

This is the hatred for opposing views that Scientology instills in its members.

Any tendency to be judgmental, confrontational or hostile toward someone is eventually only amplified by Scientology. As hurtful as it was to read those things from the mother of my daughter, I knew who and what was really behind it, and it wasn't really Erica.

On April 11, 2012 Hillary Holten died at Narconon Arrowhead. She had a condition called congenital adrenal hyperplasia and her parents were allegedly assured by Narconon staff that they were medically equipped to be able to help her, though she died the day after she checked in. The state medical examiner was unable to identify an exact cause of death for her.

As soon as I saw the news, I called Erica and told her that I wanted to be sure she wasn't using my last name anymore on anything she does related to Narconon. She had been using Catton for most things so she would have the same last name as Ella. She said she didn't know what I was talking about, but that she didn't want to have any conversation with me about anything relating to Narconon or Scientology since I was labeled as a suppressive.

I also found out that Costas Raikos died of a drug overdose that same month. He was a former staff member at Arrowhead and former son-in-law to Vicki Smith.

At the end of June news broke that Katie Holmes had filed for divorce from Tom Cruise and was seeking full custody. I had really hoped that this would be an indicator for Erica since she looked up to Katie in a way and Suri was just a year older than Ella, but it was never discussed.

Just a few days later, I was on vacation with Ella and my brother's family for the 4th of July when news broke of the drug overdose death of Alexander Jentzsch. He was the son of missing Church of Scientology International President Heber Jentzsch. Heber had been locked up in The Hole with Rena and others, but was paraded out for his son's funeral. Alexander's mother is Karen de la Carriere, who was a highly-trained auditor by L. Ron Hubbard who had also spoken out against the church's abuses and was subsequently declared an SP as well. She hadn't seen her son in a while due to forced disconnection and wasn't even allowed to attend his funeral. I felt for her, deeply, and couldn't imagine what that must have been like. It also reaffirmed my vow to myself that I would tell Ella the truth of the whole matter before being indoctrinated by the church to try and keep her away from me.

Erica and I had very limited contact after that, and later in July arranged a new calendar through the end of this school year. That was the last time we spoke or had any direct email or text. She removed me as a contact on her phone and blocked me from seeing anything on her Facebook. Any pictures posted I have to get through my mother or her mother.

Erica eventually completely cut off all contact, and hired a young woman to relay any and all communication between us.

The church calls it "using a via". She does occasionally forward a picture or video of a special event through this other woman, but nothing has been sent directly since July of 2012. This via is also used to escort my daughter between the car and the airport when I fly in to pick her up and fly her back, or to and from the hotel when I go down there to visit.

I can only reach my five year old daughter on her own phone - if she feels like answering or calling. It is built into the agreement that I get a written update every Friday and she makes sure Ella calls at least twice per week. Thankfully Ella likes talking to me and we call each other more often than that, but this has been a heartbreaking year, especially considering how much time we used to spend together since I have worked from home her entire life.

If this continues on too much longer, the time will come when she will be approached by Scientologists about Hubbard's SP doctrine. It has to come to a stop.

12 DECIDING TO SPEAK OUT

Since I had been following the developments of the church and Narconon online through various forums, blogs and media outlets, I was very much in tune with what was going on. One day someone on Reaching for the Tipping Point posted scanned documents of depositions in the Estate of Patrick Desmond vs. Narconon of Georgia and Narconon International case. I read where Mary Rieser, Clark Carr and others blatantly lied under oath.

Hubbard made it a High Crime (Suppressive Act) within Scientology to cooperate with any government agency or civil inquiry or speak out publicly against the church, affiliated organization or individual Scientologists. He wanted it kept quiet and advised members to tell "acceptable truths" (only half-lies), which is what most of the rest of their statements were comprised of.

They are taught to believe that anyone who is critical of them or any Hubbard-related activity are automatically bad and so it's okay to try and deceive them to protect the group. Despite my understanding of those policies and my own history dealing with them, I was appalled how both they knowingly altered the truth to cover for the organization's dangerous practices and the fact of the control that the church of Scientology has over Narconon.

Then, on July 19, 2012 Stacy Dawn Murphy died at the Narconon Arrowhead facility of what autopsy results later concluded to be a drug overdose. She was the third death at

Narconon Arrowhead in nine months.

NBC's *Rock Center* with Brian Williams had covered stories related to the abuse and fraud in Scientology earlier in the summer, and show producers were quick to jump on the story in Oklahoma. On Thursday, August 16th, they aired a story about the deaths at Arrowhead, including interviews with Stacy's parents and others. I decided that night I needed to say something publicly, not just comment on blogs or message boards under an unknown handle.

I had written several variations of an extremely condensed version of events leading up to my departure from Narconon and Scientology, but never posted any of them in full anywhere or under my name. I spent a good portion of the next day writing a new statement. By Friday night I had posted my first public statement.

Saturday morning I notified Marty Rathbun of my post, as well as Tony Ortega. Within the hour Tony had revealed my situation and that I had spoken to him previously as a source of information about Arrowhead just a week or so prior.

I then took off and went to Six Flags theme park with a friend, and spent the rest of the day trying to relax and have fun, but I was filled with great anxiety as I began to get all kinds of feedback through the Village Voice readers' comments, comments on my own blog and direct messages through email and Facebook.

A few days later I did an interview via Skype with the Fox affiliate in Oklahoma City regarding Narconon Arrowhead, though only a small portion of it was used.

The majority of feedback I got was very positive and supportive of what I was doing. A few people weren't so happy. One Arrowhead staff member wrote, "I have worked for Narconon for 4 years and havent touched scientology, that was ur choice ASSHOLE!! UR Decision. UR Move. Ur Responsibility, U backed out, u fucked it up, u decided to take the spot light and didnt uphold your duties. U are a waterdownversion of a coward who is sobbing over a bad divorce and trying to find a childish way to cope with it."

To which I replied, "[Staff member] if you read the whole thing you would have seen that 1) I have never meant you nor anyone of my friends there any harm, 2) There is way, way more to the entire story, and 3) Just by the virtue of applying the principals of the program and those of being a staff member there (conditions, TRs, etc.) you ARE practicing Scientology, you just believed when you were told it's not."

I was also contacted by two other former staff members, both of whom were still connected to Narconon and/or Scientology in a big way. One completely condemned me but alluded to knowing the church is screwed up, while the other was asking for a bit of help yet still disconnecting. I found it very odd.

About a week after the *Rock Center* feature, and a few days after I spoke out, Gary Smith issued an open letter stating Narconon Arrowhead's position. A few things stood out for me that he knew were blatant lies and/or "acceptable truths", and as before, I'm sure it was reviewed by OSA before going out to the media.

One of the things Smith wrote was, "Narconon Arrowhead is certified to offer non medical detox services by the ODMHSAS and accredited by CARF and has complied fully with all applicable regulations and treatment standards set forth by these two agencies. Additionally, Narconon has remained in full compliance with all state laws that govern the legal operation and conduct of a Drug and Alcohol Rehabilitation Program in Oklahoma since it was first licensed and accredited in 1992."

This is untrue. Not only was he actively engaged in trying to get Narconon Arrowhead acceptable and into compliance, but was trying to change the law because he knew it wasn't. The plan they eventually concocted was to work out sort of a "don't ask, don't tell" situation by only getting the withdrawal portion of the program certified by the state and having them accept CARF accreditation for the remainder. Why only get the non-medical detox certified and not the rest of the program?

In addition, Oklahoma Law states in Title 43A that "All claims by and accomplishments publicized by any applicant for certification or any certified alcohol- or drug-dependent organization, including but not limited to consumer count and success rates, shall be documented and verifiable by the Board."

Narconon has never been able to prove its published success rate and certainly hasn't presented any evidence to the State Board of Mental Health and Substance Abuse Services.

Gary also stated some staff credentials, claiming that they had three Licensed Alcohol and Drug Counselors (LADCs). One of them was his wife Vicki, and the other two were unidentified. I surmised they were Rev. James McLaughlin and Kent McGregor, neither of whom has ever been on staff at Arrowhead, though they may get paid as consultants. The database of licensed counselors doesn't show anyone else in the area of Narconon in Oklahoma, which is why I believed it to be Kent and James.

Smith announced that he had 20 Certified Chemical Dependency Counselors (CCDCs), but he knows these are not valid certifications in the state of Oklahoma, let alone the fact of what I shared earlier about how many of us got our certifications back in 2004.

Gary proclaimed that, "While most of the principals and rehabilitation methods used at Narconon can be found within the vast amount of information contained in the religion of Scientology materials, all of the materials pertaining to the Narconon recovery program have been completely secularized and contain no religious philosophy."

This is the biggest lie of all. It is based only upon L. Ron Hubbard's religious philosophy - every step. None of it comes from any outside source other than him, so Smith actually contradicts himself within the same sentence because it is true that it can all be found in Scientology materials.

In November Gary Smith issued another statement to the media regarding the recent deaths that included, "…Narconon was not in any way responsible for these deaths and it fully intends to aggressively defend these claims in the courts." Smith had lied yet again, as he had issued the executive briefing for fundraising years earlier that included direct statements proving that he was fully aware of the legal liability for students arriving on the property, whether there was an attempt to transfer them to another healthcare facility or not.

A handful of former and even current Narconon staff members began contacting me for various reasons, either to provide information or lend support. Some were referred through other outspoken sources, and more continue to step forward and provide information. Meanwhile, the vast majority of Narconon staff and Scientologists remain silent about what is going on, presumably because they are still under insane pressure to make as much money as possible and not look at anything negative said about them. They are also threatened with losing their jobs if they are caught communicating to outspoken critics.

There are currently many pending lawsuits against Narconon centers, Narconon International and even ABLE. Some of the suits are for negligence and wrongful death, others for fraud or something else. In the past most lawsuits against Narconon centers were fairly quickly dealt with, if not at least quietly settled. However, not only is there a growing movement of people sharing information online such as public record court documents, but there is also the increased rate of associated deaths. This is truly disturbing and the details of these are easily available online.

The main reason that so many of them go away quietly is because Scientology and Narconon lawyers often settle with non-disclosure agreements stating that in order for the victims to receive their money they agree to not speak of the terms of the settlement publicly at all.

That trend looked like it was going to change with the Desmond case in Georgia, but Narconon wound up being able to settle late Friday night before jury selection for the trial was going to begin the following Monday. The family and their team of attorneys led by Jeff Harris and Rebecca Franklin were extremely diligent and were able to uncover a lot of damning evidence, despite repeated attempts by Narconon of Georgia and Narconon International to lie, hide evidence and continue to be deceptive. I was set to testify in the case voluntarily regarding the activities of the Narconon network given my years of involvement at many levels. I was not being paid anything to appear or assist with the plaintiff's attorneys. I was helping because I felt it was the right thing to do, as so many other people were doing.

Narconon of Georgia is still under appeal at this time to operate in the state after notice was given to them that their license was being revoked. Mary Rieser resigned as the Executive Director. She was replaced by Jeannie Trahant.

Former U.S. prosecutor Gary Richardson and his multiple

plaintiffs are up next in Oklahoma, and we'll see where it goes from there. There are still ongoing investigations in Oklahoma by state agencies as well, with the possibility of criminal charges for negligence in addition to the civil suits. Oklahoma Senator Tom Ivester has also introduced legislation that would amend the current rehab certification laws to try and have tighter restriction on Narconon in the state.

It looks like this really is the beginning of the end for Narconon and Scientology. There are too many mounting civil lawsuits and there are inevitable criminal charges looming from the blatant mistreatment and deception of people. There are also an increasing number of people waking up, walking away and speaking out through books, media, blogs, forums and other ways.

Their only hope, in my opinion, is to shed the inhumane procedures that have left them in these situations and that have harmed so many people. Narconon either needs to come clean and say it is a faith-based organization or it needs to comply with recognized treatment practices and oversight. A failure to do either one of those will only be further deception and will result in continuing facility closures and bankruptcy for Narconon International. The network will be disbanded and individual centers will be scrambling to stay open by changing their names and getting rid of anything associated with the word Narconon.

CONCLUSIONS

From all of this, as it is still unfolding, I have some understandings as well as my own theories about various parts. I have no doubt that I have unintentionally missed important details or events, but I have certainly tried to tell all that I know about what has happened regarding Narconon and Scientology. Prior to this I had tried to block out so much of it due to the tremendous sting of realizing most of it was based on lies and manipulation, and that I not only fell for it but perpetuated it. It is quite a shock to recover from, but I am doing so each week.

I am very thankful for all of those people who have come forward to either publicly take a stand or collectively work to share information so that the truth sees the light of day. I hope that I am able to have an impact on helping others wake up as well.

What happened to Rena? Given that she was apologetic for the lifestyle of David Miscavige and the way she took control of situations, I believe that Miscavige saw her as a threat. She is strong-willed and many years in the Int RPF will break someone down into a malleable shell of a person willing to do the bidding of Miscavige and the church. I find it difficult to understand why her husband would allow it to continue and I hope that their entire family makes it out soon. She's been out of the public eye for nearly six years now, and I think the next place she surfaces will be out of the Sea Org like Tommy Davis, whether she shares her experiences openly or not.

As for Narconon, it absolutely isn't a legitimate addiction treatment center. It can't be. It is a faith-based program composed entirely of Scientology principles and techniques. That is the only category it should be allowed to operate in, if at all, as it is bound by L. Ron Hubbard's teachings and policies and therefore not able to change. In fact, it should actually be prosecuted for continuing to promote a false success rate at the very least, because they have never been able to produce anywhere near the results they repeatedly claim.

Was I ever really a true addict? No. Despite my assertion of such over the years to try and gain acceptance in the addiction treatment field, I wasn't. There is a reason why there are different levels of diagnoses by real professionals. I pretended to know more about addiction than I really did, just like Narconon does. Scientologists are taught to display certainty, whether they really are correct or not. I have since met with real professionals who have explained the differences.

It has taken a lot of personal introspection to realize that I am not an addiction expert and never was, but I have collected some valuable information along the way and believe some of my opinions are still valid based on actual experience. I know that I have a lot more to learn though and that my opinions can change with new information. That is part of the beauty of evolution of thought and a luxury that Scientologists don't have since they are confined to the parameters drawn by Hubbard.

Like many parents, mine did what they could to try and help. They accepted bad advice given to them by a couple of Scientologists. They fell for the same scam that so many parents do all over the world with Narconon each day.

Regarding my marriage, I know without a doubt that Erica is actually a wonderful person and a great mother. I miss being a family, though I definitely do not miss the fighting. The disagreements, upsets and difficulties we had were only amplified by Scientology in the long run, not helped by it. It has been my observation that the divorce rate in Scientology is actually much higher than most other belief systems and social groups. I hope that one day she will be free from their influence and find peace within herself as I am trying to do now. I hope she can break away from the mental confines that Scientology places within the mind of a True Believer. I wish her happiness, whether it is with Oliver or someone else in the future.

Scientologist groups have their own version of McCarthyism, but with different levels or layers. Rather than being labeled as a Communist, Scientologists like to label people as out-ethics, disaffected or an SP - in descending order from bad to worst. I eventually worked my way down to the lowest of levels in their eyes. What were my crimes? As L. Ron Hubbard himself would have said – my only crimes were being there and communicating.

What I really did was completely devote all aspects of my life for more than a decade to this group, via Narconon drug prevention and rehabilitation and directly with Scientology and its various churches, fundraising campaigns and volunteer activities. The same qualities that helped me stand out as a leader amongst my peers in that group - an ability to create and perceive, to communicate and to uphold high standards - were the same things that got me declared as an SP. I observed harmful things being committed by Scientology through the church and Narconon, communicated about them, and refused to accept things that I knew were incorrect or not okay. In short, I was attacked for trying to do the right thing, so I guess getting labeled an SP is actually at the high end of the scale in the real world.

Narconon and Scientology originally appealed to my natural altruistic tendencies. I like helping others and seeing them be happy, especially children. I fell for the illusion that Scientology would ultimately produce eternal knowledge and happiness for everyone. They used my own goodwill against me, as they have done with so many others.

In my opinion, Scientology is a dangerous, thought-controlling organization that was the creation of one man and his narcissistic delusions. Whatever desire Hubbard had to help others was eventually trumped by his desire to have people under his control, just like whatever positives I experienced in the group were overshadowed by the negatives. I absolutely do not wish for anyone else to get sucked into the trap, especially not my daughter.

I believe the only true EP of Scientology is to no longer adhere to it, as we have seen even among the breakaway movement of Independent Scientologists. These are people who have evolved enough to be able to pick and choose what parts, if any, make sense to them and discard those that they feel are hindering their freedoms socially, mentally, spiritually or otherwise.

I definitely do not consider myself a Scientologist in any form and have zero intentions of following anything that came from Hubbard, but I do support freedom of religion, thought, philosophy and practice, as long as people are not harming others as a result of their beliefs.

I have learned some incredibly valuable lessons through this entire ordeal, and I have paid some hefty prices for the experience. It is not over. I am continuing to evolve. I have become much more accepting and tolerant of others, especially as I see how even good-hearted and intelligent people can get caught up in something that is destructive.

The healing process as been taking much longer than I originally anticipated, but reading others' stories in places like the Ex-Scientologist Message Board (ESMB) helped a lot. I've also gotten back to reading and writing things that bring enjoyment and creativity again. I quit smoking a year ago as well. Things continue to get better in most areas, and soon there will be a full recovery. Thank you for taking the time to read my story, as this is certainly part of that recovery.

Since all of this is continuing to unfold, I will be posting updates at www.haveyoutoldall.com, in addition to some pictures relating to the book and commentary on things happening with both Narconon and Scientology. There is a long way to go for the full truth to come out, people to be freed and justice to prevail.